Dating
Dress rehearsal
for DIVORCE

FRANK & LISA ARMSTEAD

iUniverse, Inc.
Bloomington

Dating
Dress rehearsal for Divorce

iUniverse books may be ordered through booksellers or by contacting:

iUniverse
1663 Liberty Drive
Bloomington, IN 47403
www.iuniverse.com
1-800-Authors (1-800-288-4677)

ISBN: 978-0-595-52456-3 (sc)
ISBN: 978-0-595-62508-6 (e)

Printed in the United States of America

iUniverse rev. date: 10/10/2011

This book is dedicated to our two beautiful children, Joel Christopher and Rhema Christian. You are a blessing from God and a great joy to have in our lives. We love you and desire only God's best for you. Joel, you are full of compassion and have the heart of God. Rhema, you are filled with a relentless passion for what you desire, you both will experience His Kingdom. Although you have two different personalities, God will use you both greatly. We pray these principles will one day help prepare you for the person that God will eventually send your way, while you advance His Kingdom. We Love You.

•

And
To the memory of our dear friend Monique Eniola Emdin.
We love you

We thank Gloria Hasley for editing

Contents

Forward

It has been my privilege to pastor both Frank and Lisa for over seventeen years, as well as do their wedding about fifteen years ago. I have seen them mature, and grow into the couple we know today. In addition, we have had the opportunity of working together in fulltime ministry for over 10 years.

The Armstead's are a shining example of one couple, who I personally know, who did it God's way! While we all know the value of abstinence before marriage, not many have practiced this principal to get the benefits. Many have allowed the attitudes of secular society to invade the church where we have had to witness the shipwrecked lives of our youth and young adults. We see our people having babies out of wedlock, contracting diseases, and being bound by souls ties, just to name a few of the perils. How long will this be the testimony of the church?

The true power of the gospel is not just in preaching, but it is in practice. I have been blessed by watching their lives, character, and integrity as they live and minister to others, in particular the couples whose lives they have personally touched. I have seen couples prosper and be blessed as they have followed the godly counsel Frank and Lisa have freely shared.

The Bible tells us, through King Solomon, not to wake love before its time. There is a need for us to understand there is a godly way to have friendship and relationship, with those of the opposite sex, without defiling one another. I know Frank and Lisa will help us maneuver this very sensitive and difficult area. Therefore, I highly recommend Dating: Dress Rehearsal for Divorce because by following these insightful guidelines individuals can expect to reap definite benefits in their personal life, and their relationship. This book can be used as a practical guide to help young, and old alike, make the right decisions that will positively impact their future. After reading this book, as individuals decide to get married they are sure to find they are well equipped with the necessary tools for success.

Bishop-Elect Michael A. Badger

Introduction

Whether we realize it or not, being single is a part of life that we all will experience at some point during our lifetime. How we maneuver our way through being single is often times shaped by our observations and opinions of family, friends, peers, our belief system, media and our experiences throughout our life.

Some may experience being single once, and others may experience being single multiple times during their life. How an individual feels about being single will also shape in part what they do with being single. How one thinks about being single will determine, in part, if they embrace their singleness, or try to escape from it with earnest. If the truth be told about being single it is one of the greatest opportune times in an individual's life for self development, preservation and planning.

We discovered early, as I am sure you and everyone else has discovered, that God does not specifically address dating in the Scriptures. For the purposes of our conversation, He does, however, address two groups of people, they are brothers and sisters in Christ and husbands and wives. For brothers and sisters in Christ, everything outside of husbands and wives in the sixty six books applies. This includes the Ten Commandments, The Beatitudes, The Golden Rule, every parable, and every scenario. For husbands and wives everything within the sixty-six books applies. For each group are parameters for successful everyday living. This we also believe includes relationship development and marriage preparation. For married individuals, it is necessary to keep in the forefront of our mind, we are first brothers and sisters in Christ. While this is quite the paradigm shift for many, it establishes clear relational guidelines.

Whether we plan to remain single until a certain age, certain accomplishments in life, or until a certain someone comes along we have to examine the bridge that takes us from being single to being married. Will this bridge be like the Brooklyn Bridge, as stable as the ground we walk? Or will this bridge be more like an obstacle course only intended to take us from one side to the other? One bridge offers a generous amount of ease, stability, peace of mind and assurance. The other bridge, the equivalent anxiety of sudden death on a live mine field with great and measurable toil. We each must personally ask at the appropriate time what bridge will cross us over from being single to being married? Will I know when I've found it? How do I cross it? For those who may be actively pursing the option of marriage, or are prudently considering it at some point, this is what Dating: Dress Rehearsal for Divorce is all about. We would like to look at two different bridges, or models, that take you in the direction of marriage.

A favorite scripture of ours reminds us that God is interested in every aspect of our lives going well. This includes relationships too.

> *I desire above all things that you prosper*
> *and be in good health even as your soul prospers.*
> 3 John 2

The word *prosper* really refers to the word *journey*. While we are on our journey through life His desire is that everything go well for us. This includes relationships, career, family, finances, health, and everything else that pertains to us. God doesn't just want to know that we can pray five hours a day and fast 20 days out of the month. He wants to know that we are getting along well in what we do when we get up from prayer. This scripture encourages and reminds us that God really loves us, and is concerned about every aspect of our lives while we are on this journey through life.

We have noticed, and you too may have noticed, that when people are not doing well in their relationships it generally affects other areas of their life. This is true whether people are married or single, a child or adult, young or old. Whether it is between a boss and employee, parent and a child, husband and wife, or a brother and sister it does affect our lives. Why is this so? Relationships are a significant part of who we are as human beings because God has created us to be relational. We have been created in God's image *and* in His likeness. This is how God Himself is; He is relational. That is why He desires relationship and not just religion from us. There is an innate part of us that needs to give and receive communication, companionship, and interaction with others. Thus, relationships really do have the potential of steering an individual's destiny. When we get it right, it can be worth our weight in gold; if not it can be the noose around our neck cutting off the very breath of life from us.

We therefore have spent a considerable amount of time with both non-married and married couples, and have had to seek the wisdom of God concerning not just dating and being married, but also the little grey areas in between. This has led us to the Word of God to really find out what God's perspective is about crossing over on the right bridge to the desired destination.

Over the years one of the largest areas of relationship challenges that we have seen is that of husband and wives where issues resurface and arise because they did not fully prepare and evaluate their situations and count the cost. The Word of God clearly asks

> *For which of you, intending to build a tower, sit*
> *Not down first, and counteth the cost, whether*
> *He have sufficient to finish it?*
> *Luke 14:28*

Pastoral Premarital Counseling is one proactive approach to this. When couples from our church plan to get married the first prerequisite is to complete the thirteen week minimum premarital course. This course challenges the couple to think beyond just being in love, and more intently about aspects pertaining to both individuals and their future spouse. As well, they are challenged to evaluate the timing and direction of their relationship. Each session is scheduled two weeks to one month a part so the couple can digest everything they have received while they further process and reflect on everything through various assignments.

You may not be too surprised to find out that most people spend more time and resources investing in their wedding day and honeymoon arrangements than they do to invest in their marriage. You may, however, be a little bit more surprised to find out that more people spend a greater amount of time preparing for their drivers license test than they do preparing to be married to a someone for the rest of their life.

The premarital preparation process most definitely equips couples with tools they will eventually need. We always let couples know it's not a matter of *if* you will need the tools, but it's a matter of *when* you will need your tools. For some couples, it's sooner than later, and for others it's later than sooner. Either way, it is good to know that the person you are with has the same bag of tools and is willing to use them so you can build together.

Ideally, we like to start with singles while they are still *single*, before they become emotionally attached to someone. We like to give them the tools for the process of making good, sound and grounded choices before their hearts become involved. We encourage youth and adults everywhere who are serious about connecting with their person of destiny to investigate, not just date. Haphazard dating is merely a dress rehearsal for disappointment, disaster and the possibility for divorce when your heart is involved before your head.

This is what concerns us about the whole concept of internet and cyber dating. We strongly caution people, particularly youth, because there is no way of knowing what you are really getting yourself into. Cyber dating provides more opportunities for predators to disguise themselves and their motives. They are better able to present themselves as everything you are looking for and not necessarily what they really are.

We have seen too many times where couples come in our office with wedding dates already set, dresses already bought, bridesmaids selected, and deposits on cakes, and initials etched in crystal and silverware. Everything was pretty much final. This was all regardless of what the pastoral counseling revealed; if the couple knew each other well enough or not, compatible or not, equally yoked or not, or had issues or not. They were in love, and to them that was the greatest determining factor. However, we strongly discourage beginning the premarital pastoral counseling process with a date already selected. We find when it is not done in this order the couple does not as readily step back to prudently evaluate the realities of their relationship with the necessary resolves. Once dates are already set, we hear a lot more couples answer issues with things like, "we're fine with it", " I can live with that", "s/he or I will get over it", "it's not that big of a deal", and so on. For some of these couples I don't think Jesus Himself could have convinced them otherwise. We always find it interesting that the un-churched, who come to us, often times take the premarital process more seriously than those who feel they are required to do it.

People often like to ask us about how we did it. They see the happily ever after but they did not see the beginning chapters of our story together. One of us is loud, and the other is quiet. One of us sees in black and white, and the other sees in techni-color. One of us plays it safe, and the other is risky and loves a good adventure. Furthermore, the truth is we really didn't do everything the way we recommend to others today. We didn't have our credit together, didn't complete school first, and we were both still very young. We thank God for His grace, but we could have made our way a lot easier had we listened to people, finished preparing ourselves, and had a little more personal development and business in order. We loved each other (and still do) but some of the pressures that we experienced didn't necessarily have to be a part of our experience together. Several things could have been done differently. In fact we wish we had, then, the wealth of knowledge and experience that we now share with others. Back then our premarital counseling was all of a half an hour to prepare us for a whole lifetime together. Because of our experiences and what we see others experiencing, it gives us a great passion for preparing and helping couples. We desire that every couple have all the help and resources of heaven and earth available to them.

Let's face it in grade school we only learned three of the four R's; R-reading, R-writing and R- arithmetic. Most of us did not get the fourth "R"; relationships! Not even in Sunday School and Vacation Bible School was dating and courting squeezed in with the Ten Commandments, the Lord's

Prayer, and the Beatitudes. We were just told "don't do it", which we have to admit is a little more than what young people in church were sometimes told.

Without practical help, we believe people learn one of two ways; either you live and learn or you enroll in the school of hard knocks. There may be a band aide available if you stump your toe, or hit your head, but it's just much better to not need a band aide in the first place. With great anticipation and excitement, we desire to share the truths of our findings with you.

This is what we hope this book will do for you. It is our prayer that through this book we can help you cross the bridge without stumping your toe or hitting your head, by giving practical tools and maneuvering strategies based on the principles of the Word of God. Hopefully, this will also turn on some lights as you walk the hallways of life so you don't get lost in the corridors of bad relationships and wrong decisions.

Dating: Dress Rehearsal for Divorce has been designed particularly with the non-married person in mind who desires to cross this bridge to get from one side to the next, with as little anxiety as possible. This book is the result of many years of meeting with a countless number of people and gathering some "if I knew back then" type of information. We really believe you will enjoy the practical wisdom of this book, and will refer back to it many times over. Do we have all the answers? No, but we would like to share with you what we do have.

This book looks at three different types of relationships: dating, courting and engagement. The premise of Dating: Dress Rehearsal for Divorce is to understand the benefits of courting in lieu of dating. This book critically looks at the practices and habits of dating verses courting along with the objectives of engagement as the final step toward marriage. In reading Dating: Dress Rehearsal for Divorce, we encourage you to critically look at the practices, purposes, responses and responsibilities of each along with what they perpetuate, persuade, and prepare you for.

Dating in and of itself is not necessarily a bad thing. One has to look at their own objective. After you evaluate your objective, it is equally important to find out if the other party has the same objective as you. Finally look at where it is taking you. Is the other person and relationship headed in the same direction as your destiny?

Dating is not designed to bring about the results of a lasting relationship. It is a short cut to fulfill real and permanent desires that God has created within each of us. Courting on the other hand uses time (in really getting to know an individual) as a resource to maximize future time in bringing fulfillment to the same intrinsic desires.

The main thought mechanism of dating is the heart with emphasis on the right now, image, personality, and appearances. The main thought mechanism for courting is the head with emphasis on planning and preparations for future dividends made payable in fulfillment of destiny and longevity in the relationship. Therefore truth, character, and integrity become the sought after commodities of courting. Courting, we believe, also helps perpetuate two whole and complete individuals with a greater potential of establishing and building a lasting relationship.

We definitely believe this book will be helpful to you as you desire to cross your own personal bridge. Remember who you connect with will be one of the most crucial decisions you make in your life. It may mean the difference between destiny or depression, possibly life or death. Ask yourself the question "can I afford to miss it in this area of my life"?

PART 1

In All Thy Getting Get An Understanding
What It's All About

*Wisdom is the principal thing; therefore get
wisdom: and with all thy getting get understanding.
Proverbs 4:7*

*He that getteth wisdom loveth his own soul:
he that keepeth understanding shall find good.
Proverbs 19:8*

*Through wisdom is a house builded;
and by understanding it is established:
Proverbs 24:3*

Our Story

Today when we talk to couples they often ask "What is your story? Tell us what you did. How did you do it?" When we got married we were both virgins. A concept equated with the dinosaurs, but definitely not extinct. Let me say right off the bat, as we mentioned in the Introduction, we did not do it then how we recommend to couples today. However, we can say we would have done some things differently and in different timing if we had the same information available to us. We do believe there is more information and teaching available than when we dated, and think that you actually have a better chance than we did at making it and doing it right. While keeping yourself is important, it is definitely not the only needful factor. And it, alone, certainly does not mean you are ready or equipped for a marriage.

For us, well we did it how God says to do it, as much as we knew to do. And you can do it too, if you choose to do what God says. That is the bottom line, there is no secret formula and no special grace.

Nonetheless, our "story" is one that we don't mind sharing, but it is neither magical, nor earth shattering-just practical! We are confident that it is something you can do too. There were two factors we believe that made our choices to be virgins possible. One, it was our choice before we ever knew who the other was. In other words, we had a standard for our own lives that was independent of the other person. God led us to the individual that made the same choice and respected our personal decisions.

Second, because abstinence was a personal decision our actions had to be in agreement with our choice. Therefore to support our choice we did some very practical things that we will share with you toward the end of the book.

When we first met, it was in a group setting, and our relationship grew out of common fellowship with mutual friends. We didn't initially date. In fact, interest was not initially mutual. It was over the course of time and getting to know one another, learning of commonalities and goals that something more began to develop.

Because we were both in school, we *dated* each other long distance for about six years before we eventually married. However, when we did get married, I can definitely say that the decision to remain abstinent before marriage benefited our relationship. Today we have been married for more than 15 years. Our testimony is that He kept us.

We believe the challenge people face today, is the same as we did. This challenge is how to reconcile the Word of God with living in the world without compromising our standard of who we are. After all, the Bible does admonish us to be in the world but not of the world. Most of us would agree that we live in a very over-sexed society that is continuously pumping sex on television, billboards, radios, and everywhere we go. Sex sells everything from cereal to automobiles. This is the same challenge we faced growing up in the 80's.

Therefore, after assessing all that we did, even what we didn't do, one thing we agree upon, at this point, is that we do not believe the traditional sense of dating yields the best results. Although we were both virgins, there is still a lot more involved in doing what is right, appropriate, and in order than just not having sex before marriage. Therefore we again reiterate that dating is not the best model of relationship development that will benefit a healthy, strong, lasting relationship. A relationship built on the values of truth, fidelity, commitment and longevity.

For those that are already married, those who have no intentions on marrying or even re-marrying, it is never too late to be informed. Not because knowledge is power, (I personally do not believe that) rather because application of knowledge is power. In other words, it's not what you know, but what you do with what you know that will make a difference in your life -- possibly even save your life. We encourage you to share the information that may, or may not, have been available to you. Hopefully more informed decisions can be part of each of our arsenals against the enemy of our marriages, our families, our churches, and our communities. Together, hopefully we can begin to reverse some of the devastating effects of divorce by reflecting the heart and intentions of God in our relationships, marriages, families and homes.

We don't say you can do it because we did it. Rather you can do it because God makes it possible for you to do. So again, if you make up your mind, you can do it too singles, even if you start from today.

CHAPTER 1

In The Beginning
(Origin & History Of It All)

So God created man in his own image, in the image of God
created he him; male and female created he them.
Genesis 1:27

Being created in God's *image* and *likeness* not only speaks to what we should
be like. This clearly says two things to us. One, in His image means I am to
look like God. In other words, be a reflection of Him on earth. When people
see us they should also see the essence of who God is. Second, created in his
likeness means I am *to be like God*. In other words, not just look like Him, but
I am to act like Him; bring His explicit will to this earth through my attitude
and actions. As an Ambassador I transact here on earth in God's stead and
demonstrate who He is through everything I do. That's the Kingdom! One
New Testament scripture that says it all:

Thy kingdom come. Thy will be done
in earth, as it is in heaven.
Matthew 6:10

When discussing marriage we have to understand that it is the ultimate
relationship the Word of God talks about in describing our relationship with
Christ. The Church is the Bride of Christ and Christ is the Bridegroom.
Consequently, each of our individual marriages is also intended to be a
reflection of this divine marriage. In other words, all of our marriages should
look like and be like Christ's marriage with the Church. Further noted, the
bride reflects who her husband is just as the bridegroom represents who his
wife is.

Also necessary to be said about marriage is that it is intended by God for
the raising up of godly seed, as well as to advance the Kingdom Heaven here

on earth. With this said, let's look at all of this business with dating, courting, and marriage and how it fits with God's original intentions and purposes.

Dating

Can a man take fire in his bosom,
and his clothes not be burned?
Proverbs 6:27

When we look at statistics for the current divorce rate verses fifty years ago without a doubt it can be said that something is suspect about the current spousal selection process. Recognizing we did not have statistics a century ago that look like our current statistics, one may draw the obvious conclusion that things are changing. Some may say there is something seriously wrong about our current system of meeting and marrying, while others may disagree and muse that it is all we have to work with. We submit to you it is a little of both people and process. We recall having a conversation with a pastor from the Ivory Coast in reference to the American way of getting married being so easy to get into and even easier to get out of. In his country he said, you thoroughly check out the other individual, where they have been, where they are going and the family they come from. They check you out too. More people are involved in the process other than just the couple. This provides for a built in system of accountability and support surrounding the marriage.

While the dating process as we currently know it may not be the whole reason for short lived relationships and dissolving marriages, it definitely lends a great deal. People, on the other hand, are definitely marrying without the same convictions of commitment as some years ago. We are also discovering people know relatively little about the one they have said they want to spend the rest of their life with.

The whole process of *dating*, as we know it, is a fairly recent concept and has done a great deal of evolving largely just within the last century. In fact, as a twentieth century concept, it has reached its height. It's not an age old, and definitely not an age old tested concept that works. According to countless numbers of statistics it works less than 50% of the time. Prior to the twentieth century, there were not only other ways by which people were meeting and establishing the workings of lasting marital relationships, but there was also a different mindset and emphasis people had until the Era of Romanticism.

The term Romanticism comes from the medieval word for fictional literature written about love in any of the romance languages such as French, Spanish and Italian. Dating is the love child of this Eighteenth and nineteenth Century philosophy.

You more than likely studied Romanticism in History, Art or Literature class. People such as Jean-Jacques Rousseau, Emily Dickinson, Ralph Waldo Emerson and so many more are from this time period. If you remember your history lessons, Romanticism introduced the rise of individualism. Among other things, it emphasized strong emotion over intellect and re-establishing social norms and mores. It ran opposite to the grain of the previous Age of Enlightenment, resisting its focus on reason and rationale. Romanticism was weaved into the culture of the day and was present in everything from philosophy to art and from literature to politics in Western cultures. It was a great period, but it did to the Renaissance what the Beetles did to the 1960's.

Prior to the Era of Romanticism, most marriages were arranged. More importantly, it was understood that you loved the one you were with. Romanticism turned the tables and introduced a whole new concept of "marry the one you love". This, in and of itself is not bad, and we do not necessarily raise an issue with this. After all, we married the one we loved. The dilemma becomes at what point does the evolution of this concept stop particularly after one is married?

Some years ago an interesting online article by Wayne Swafford was shared with me called "The Dating Dilemna-A Brief History of Dating". It gave one account for tracing the steps of dating from the early 1800's. I believe it outlines the progression of dating based on the perceived progression of our society.

During Colonial times people grew up knowing each other in relaxed mixed gender settings such as school, church, neighborhoods and at home. Being single was frowned upon particularly for men because it was thought to be a sign of laziness. After all, they thought, the major prerequisite for taking a wife was being able to provide a house and support for a family.

Romanticism perpetuated the idea of "do what feels right". Therefore, the aftermath of the Romantic Era brought about the idea that men needed to be tamed and women were their docile opposite. This began the subtle divide between the previous way of growing up knowing and relating to those of the opposite sex in relaxed mixed gender settings.

Romantic love grew as the basis for marriage. Courtships became formal and took place in the home of the young lady's parents. This gave couples the opportunity and accountability while getting to know each other with the goal of marriage.

When the Industrial Revolution took off in developing cities, more young people were on their own working. This gave rise to a new middle class who were from less wealthy and smaller homes that did not accommodate courting. Therefore, a less formal way of courting in public became the norm as youth left their home to pursue relationships. They began *going out*. By the early 1900's, a new dimension of relationships developed as young people began dating without parental oversight, accountability, and endorsement.

Now that dating replaced courtship and it became *going out,* three dynamics were introduced. One: there was a shift in power from the young lady to the young man when she left the covering of her parents' home. Two: going out introduced a new monetary need and expectation. Three: the objective of getting to know a person was replaced by entertainment and the ability to provide for a good time. Incidentally, a combination of these three new dynamics did eventually provide an atmosphere and avenue for sexual expression to begin in dating. Boundaries were blurred and were no longer established by family or community but by individual peer groups. By the 1920's the boundaries of modesty between the sexes began to fade and the 1920's represented a period of sexual and social revolution. While virginity was the expectation, and was nice, it was no longer a necessity.

After WWII, early marriages were seen as a way of dealing with youth sexuality. However the 1960's resurfaced an increasing liberal attitude towards sex. Feminism further shaped this view along with dating. While more women were pursuing college and careers, and marrying later in life, by the 1980's there was an increasing number of college youth who were sexually active.

As times continued to changed we see how the norms for society also continue to change. This form of dating, as we know it, has become society's norm. There appears to have been a progression of courting in the parent's house to playing house.

This is why we say the current dating model essentially is the act of marriage without the protection of the commitment, accountability, or responsibility of marriage. This is very important as we move forward and discuss the differences and the results of dating versus courting.

Two of the most asked question is how do you get the opportunity to meet somebody if you don't date? And don't you get the opportunity to know who someone really is through dating? Well, think about it. We submit: with this being a twentieth and twenty-first century concept, relatively speaking being fairly new, and reviewing the divorce rate just within the twentieth century it appears that it may really not working that well anyway. At least not the way we would like to give it credit for.

Why not do what works and produces the best results. It is too emotionally draining and damaging to invest so much when the stakes are so high and the odds are stacked against you. As we have seen, some people never recover, others barely make it out.

We like to recommend opportunities for social interaction without having to be coupled up. Relaxed mixed gender groups of provide for great opportunities of meeting and hanging out with common interest people. You can enjoy the moment, have a good time, and get to know those around you, and yourself, a little better without the added pressure.

We also strongly believe that while you are doing the will of God for your life you will meet your mate in the Kingdom while they are doing the will of God in their own life. Why? What you need is in the Kingdom. Nothing is by accident in the Kingdom. It pays to be in purpose, being at the right place at the right time.

> *Whoso findeth a wife findeth a good thing,*
> *and obtains favor of the Lord.*
> *Proverbs 18:22*

The good thing about when God blesses us is it will benefit and add to us and not subtract from us. The person you have overlooked may be right in your midst. If you don't go in with an agenda per se but having fun, enjoying one another's presence and fellowshipping you never know God may just show you something that you have never seen before.

This is in fact how we met; at a social gathering. It was a small welcome back party for a mutual friend. Little did we know this same friend had been trying to connect us, and get us to meet for some time. However neither of us had any interest in meeting the other based on the over-zealous-religious-fanatic description that was given. However, sometime after meeting, it seemed like destiny to be in the right place at the right time just hanging out with friends.

When looking at dating, it offers no protection of commitment. So half way through, if I don't like you, I meet someone else; someone else looks prettier, another leg looks a lot nicer, something else looks a little more appealing -- there is no commitment to stay. While the other person may have gone on, you are stuck in a place in time with your heart still involved. This has the potential to leave the person in a deep sense of loss and despair. Further, if this cycle is repeated individuals customarily become even more dis-engendered with relationship longevity, or may carry a chip on their shoulder, and expect and perpetuate temporary relationships that have the tendency to become more and more shallow with the passing of time and each new face. It easily can become *get* before you get *gotten*. That has become the world's approach to dating.

COURTING

There is so much more criteria in selecting a potential mate other than being in love and having goose bumps. As one may desire to move toward the seriousness of marriage, there has to be more involved than just going out, having a good time, and how much is spent at the movies and dinner. One must also be able to meet the demands of marriage's responsibilities. Unlike dating, the purpose of courting is specifically designed to lead to marriage.

The components of courting are more aligned with biblical principals, perspectives, and approaches. We cannot say that courting in and of itself is strictly biblically based because it is not. It is something that has been practiced across many religious, cultural, ethnic, and caste boundaries by many cultures and ethnic groups around the world throughout time. Interestingly enough, courting is practiced by many cultures up to recent times as a means of learning a person.

Courting may be seen by some as the antiquated distant cousin to arranged marriages. I guess in some ways it can be viewed that way, but not strictly speaking. We wouldn't think of trying to sell you on the idea of arranged marriage in the 2000's. Although we will say that it has about a 90% proven success rate. It has a much greater success rate than traditional meet-and-marry marriages. One reason arranged marriages have a greater success rate is because of the foresight and the accountability of the process. Individuals are prepared in advance to be the spouse of a particular person or type of person. The truth is parents know what type of person will and will not work for their children. What do you mean? Simply put, if your family knows you will be marrying a political figure, or preacher, or doctor, or policeman, then you will be groomed and raised to be a spouse of someone in that position. You won't necessarily have to learn it after 20 or 30 years of living; you will be groomed to it. The awesome thing about this is parents know what type of person that will and will not be suitable for their child.

This is what courting does; it brings back into the equation some of the foresight and preparations for two people to walk together and agree. The focus is on the compatibility of goals, needs and mutual respect. Courting not only ensured that a son or daughter was *marrying right*, but it also ensured they were *rightly marrying*. Because courting is suppose to be a more cognitive process, everything gets laid out in black and white. You know what the other person's plans are and they are well aware of yours. I respect who you are as my brother or sister; I respect your goals and aspirations.

Also unlike dating, courting is more structured on and around beliefs and mores of the potential suitors and their families. This is why at some points in time and history there has been greater distain for intermarrying of various religious, cultures, and economic groups. We see this throughout the Old Testament where God warns against taking strange wives that will bring the influence of their gods.

Again the purpose of this process is to marry, not just to be out having a good time. Courting involves an extensive process more concerned with getting to know an individual for the purpose of establishing a lasting relationship that has the potential to go somewhere and produce something. Unlike the emphasis of Romanticism and an individual's heart, the emphasis of courting has to be the head first; the use of reason and rationale--head over heart .

Courting takes place when one has potentially identified another as being compatible to become one's spouse. Courting affords the opportunity of getting to know one another to be sure both are on the same page concerning the values, expectations, and goals of each one's life. The goal is getting to better know the individual that has been considered for marriage

Courting is not someone getting to know Sally today, Suzy tomorrow, and Jane on Friday. No. There is one individual that is being considered for marriage. One. One does not do the courting process with five different people. At that point it is just *dating*, where you are right back to no commitment and trying people out.

While Genesis 24 is an example of an arranged marriage we also see several significant aspects of courting when Abraham sent his servant to find a wife suitable for his son Isaac.

But you shall go to my country and to my
Family, and take a wife for my son Isaac.
Genesis 24:4

Abraham was familiar with his son, his situation and his destiny enough to know what type of wife was and was not suitable for Isaac. He gave his servant specific instructions on where to find his son's wife because he was also familiar with the background of the people.

And the damsel was very fair to look upon,
a virgin, neither had any man known her...
Genesis 24:16

This scripture lists three things about Rebekah. One she was attractive. She kept her self up and took care with her personal appearance. When the right person came she was already ready. Second, she was a virgin. Third, she was not known by a man. In other words she wasn't at the watering well playing patty cake with the men, and she wasn't tasting everyone's lemonade. She maintained her integrity

> *...and she went down to the well, and*
> *filled her pitcher, and came up.*
> Genesis 24:16

Even before the servant found Rebekah she, too, was doing something with life – she was working.

> *...the man took a golden earring ...*
> *and two bracelets for her hands...*
> *Genesis 24:22*

He had something to offer her. The point is not the jewelry, it self, rather it represented his substance to demonstrate his ability to take on the responsibility of a wife.

> *And the damsel ran, and told them of her*
> *mother's house these things.*
> *Genesis 24:28*

Rebekah quickly went home and told her family everything that was going on.

> *And the man came into the house...Genesis 24:32*
> *...I will not eat until I have told mine errand*
> *Genesis 24:33*

He did not play games. He went to meet Rebekah's family and made his intentions clear to them before making himself comfortable with their daughter, in their house, and with the situation.

> *And they blessed Rebekah and said to her,*
> *"Our sister, may you increase to thousands*
> *upon thousands; may your offspring possess*
> *the gates of their enemies."*
> *Genesis 24:60*

Before Rebekah left the covering of her family and home she left with the blessing of her family to marry Isaac.

Now Isaac had come from the way of the well Lahai Roi;
for he dwelt in the south country.
Genesis 24:62

As Isaac had reached manhood and ready for the responsibility of a wife he was not still living under the security and provision of his father's tent.

And Isaac went out to meditate in the field at the eventide:...,
Genesis 24:63

Isaac was not out lounging around with nothing to do. He was actively involved in his own personal relationship with God prior to a wife coming along side of him.

...and when she saw Isaac, she lighted off the camel...
For she said unto the servant "What man is this
that walketh in the field to meet us?...
Genesis 24:64-65

Remembering her purpose for being there was to be a wife to Isaac Rebekah, being a wise woman, humbled herself and came down off her camel. This act displayed her willingness to show submission, grace, and hospitality to her betrothed Isaac. She also used discretion in the situation by inquiring about the man approaching. She did not take it upon herself to get in Isaac's face, but she waited for the servant to present her as the treasure that was sought after and found just for him.

...therefore she took a veil, and covered herself.
Genesis24:65

Rebekah showing great respect for custom, Isaac, and herself exercised modesty by covering herself.

Isaac brought her into his mother Sarah's tent,
and took Rebekah. And she became his wife;
and he loved he:and Isaac was comforted after his mother's death.
Genesis 24:67

Isaac having a place to take Rebekah made her his wife and he loved her. It doesn't say anything about them dating, they didn't go out for coffee, lunch, or burgers. There wasn't any dating, cooking, or midnight patty cake prayer meetings but he loved her and was comforted by her

These few scriptures in Genesis 24 speak volumes. Isaac had never seen Rebekah a day before in his life, but the Bible says Isaac took her and she became his wife. Then the text says that he loved her. Not he loved her and married her, but he married her and loved her. This helps identify love as a choice.. In the text he loved her, even though he didn't date her. Abraham knew his son so well that he knew what type of wife would be suitable for Isaac. All of this was before someone thought up eharrmony.com.

With the idea of love being a choice we believe happiness has become a little overrated in today's society. Don't misunderstand. God wants us to be happy and have life and have it more abundantly. We are aware of all of that, but He also desires that we not take the carriage covenant lightly. If the truth be told, in the marriage relationship there will be days that you may not feel like being bothered with your spouse. However, that is not a license to walk away. Happiness has become the pivotal point for many fickle decisions. This is where we remember that marriage is a covenant between three: God, a husband and a wife. In essence, what we are saying when we make that choice to walk away from a covenant relationship is that because of my unhappiness something must be wrong with God's institution and system of marriage. Let us inform you that nothing is wrong with God's system.

ENGAGEMENT

Engagement is the covenant of agreeing to marry. At the point that one reaches engagement, they are making a public declaration that they have found the person they want to pursue destiny with and are interested in building a life with through a marriage covenant. Through the process of courting, individuals have recognized they have similar goals and are on the same pathway in life.

The purpose for the engagement is to prepare for both wedding and marriage, but mostly the marriage. Far too often we see couples put more prep work and time into the actual wedding day without properly preparing for the marriage. However, we believe this is the designated time to make preparations for both. The wedding represents several things. It is not just the day the bride dresses up like a princess and marries the man of her dreams. It is a public profession, before witnesses, of the commitment and covenant that the two are making before God to become one. The wedding ceremony is the celebration of the joining of two individuals that will live their lives together to see that purpose and destiny is fulfilled in both lives. A wedding also reminds us of God's desire that a man and woman be joined together just as Christ is returning for His bride, the Church. Therefore the wedding is not just a formality but has great purpose in the ceremony and sanctity of the wedding. Particularly note worthy for a wedding ceremony are the many symbolic, original, and sacred meanings of the ceremony.

Far too often we see women plan their wedding with their girlfriends, sisters, and mother. We encourage both parties to have a hand in the planning process. This is also a great opportunity to really work and plan something together. Further, there is a lot involved in planning and coordinating everything from location, to people, to menus. There are a great number of wedding planning books, software, websites and even event planning services that are available to help you. Our two biggest cautions are to stay in budget, and remember the greatest amount of preparation still goes to being ready for the marriage, and enjoying yourselves. Don't allow the planning to become a point of contention.

While marriage is a blessing, the Word of God also says it is a mystery. Taking two flesh people, no matter how in love, and making them into one flesh really is more than a notion. We envision the beautiful flowers, white dress, cake and the honeymoon night, but all of that is just one day in a life time of forever. There needs to be ample preparation for when the honeymoon is over.

Further, during engagement both parties continue to prepare and put their affairs in order to facilitate making another individual a part of their life. It almost goes without saying, but for the record, we strongly recommend that couples do not even begin to talk about marriage if they are not gainfully employed. While it may sound shallow, love does not pay bills or put food on the table. One of the top three long standing reasons for divorce is finances. That is why in dating "I love you" is too premature. You don't want to get side tracked by it; it is **not** enough to sustain a marriage. That is why it is important that you do not allow your emotions to get involved prematurely, because once your heart is in it, you are in it.

CHAPTER 2

If I Only Knew Back Then
(What It's All About)

A bishop then must be blameless, the husband
of one wife, vigilant, sober, of good behavior,
given to hospitality, apt to teach;
I Timothy 3:2

DATING

God has intended our hearts for relationships. The enemy would like nothing more than to get us hurt in relationship so we develop relationship deficiencies and are always in a needy place. This deficit will keep a person in a place of always trying to fill a void, at their own expense. Trust and all kinds of relational issues that develop try to keep us from healthy relationships.

Because a void is trying to be filled, dating almost begins to look like a game where it seems very few players ever win. My heart is with you today and my heart is with someone else tomorrow, and this goes on and on. It's almost like a (RADD) Relationship Attention Deficit Disorder. Thus, dating gets characterized by a premature investing of emotions, and also perpetuates readily changing of one's affections. This is why we choose to subtitle the book Dress Rehearsal For Divorce. Why? The habit of readily changing affections is developed. We all would agree this type of behavior is not acceptable, or anticipated, after marriage. However, many don't realize the pattern is often set during the times in our life when we start dating.

We like the way Tyler Perry puts it in his movie "Why Did I Get Married" with what they call 20/80. He said after a person is married, they do good if they can get a good 80% of an individual. He said people that leave their 80% relationship to find a 100% relationship often end up with just a 20% relationship. The idea behind this thinking is that the grass is greener on the other side. On the other side of what? Dating does not encourage or prepare an individual to get pass the surreal experience of the initial excitement of love. It is easy to try to do whatever it takes to sustain that initial feeling of excitement. Pass the passions of the moment, dinner out every night, pomp and paradise, one has to really look at what they are really getting.

We typically like to think that the one we are being true to is also being true to us. The reality is there is no obligation to commitment or to responsibility when dating. The truth is people often casually date because they don't want the commitment or responsibility of being tied to another person. Dating is an open-ended arrangement. There is always a door leading out.

We have often noticed that when people have a challenging time in a committed relationship, in particularly marriage, it's not always because of the person they are with. Sometimes there is still residue from the person who they were once connected to, or from the person who broke their heart many years ago. It is disappointing for each party involved to be with someone they really love, and who reciprocates love, but because they have a soul tie to a previous third party, it is not always easy to give all of them self. Sometimes there is that difficulty in getting pass who they left, or who left them, twenty years ago, or what was done to them in the past. The reality is they do sometimes still think about the person, they still smell their perfume or cologne because parts of that person are still resident in their soul. While they are not physically present, they are still mentally of emotionally there.

For many the evidence of dating is a broken and confused heart, from giving your heart without any reciprocated commitment. Depending on the level of involvement it is not unusual for pieces of someone else's heart to still linger with someone else even after the relationship has dissolved and everyone moves on. This can effect subsequent relationships in different ways.

These feelings, not dealt with, tend to lie dormant and get played out later. A person with soul ties is more prone to have extra marital affairs. Some materials we have read suggests that those who engage in premarital sex were more likely to engage in some type of extra marital affair.

Some of us may know of someone married who has had an affair, but we are often times not as suspect when a person has an affair of the heart. An affair of the heart is when a married person develops feelings and emotional attachments to another person outside of the marriage covenant, for whatever reason. This relationship outside of the marriage begins to meet the emotional needs of the person. This can, potentially, be more damaging, and can go on for years with only the absence of physical intimacy. Even if the relationship does not escalate to a physical relationship, it has all of the potential to. People are quicker to excuse an emotional affair saying "nothing happened". However, it still is not right especially with all the components in place for it to go all the way at any time.

Some individual's forte becomes playing cat and mouse games. They flirt, to see how far they can go without going all the way, with the idea that nothing will happen. These types of games are more often than not built on the excitement of the potential catch. Some explain this type of behavior off as "I just wanted to know if I still had it".

A crucial aspect often times overlooked in dating is that this person, I'm fooling around with, is going to become someone else's husband or wife one day. A more powerful thought than that is the idea that I will become someone else's spouse one day. Even more intense than this thought is the idea that I am going to become someone's mom or dad one day. Therefore what is done with someone before marriage, ends up becoming someone else's baggage after marriage. What is done always effects more than just the two immediate parties involved.

Dating produces all kinds of scenarios from soul ties and audacious games to affairs. Spare yourself the confusion and the heartache by using wisdom as you maneuver this area of your life. In some form or fashion soul ties is a good 80% of what we deal with when we see people. Because of people's baggage, what has happened in their past is now a part of their present, and often times their spouse and their children too. They still have a physical and/or emotional connection with someone else. Hopefully you won't be in a pastor's or therapist's office 15 years from now with these issues.

COURTING

...write the vision, and make it plan... that
He may run that readeth it.
Habakkuk 2:2

God's Word talks about the results of being unequally yoked. While spiritually we understand the principle we recognize the importance of being equally yoked in most areas of our life. This is not to say if you like basketball and I don't, it will never work. But there should be some things we have in common other than we both love Jesus. The best time to find out if you are equally yoked is before finding out that you are not equally yoked. Courting is a valuable tool for getting to know a person to help ensure you are properly yoked with who is suitable and prepared for your life. This has nothing to do with being better than somebody, but everything to do with what is best for you. Being unequally yoked often puts serious unnecessary strains on both parties, and makes walking in the same direction a toilsome task.

Genesis' account of creation is an awesome thing particularly when you get to the creation of man. We see the sovereignty of God as He displays that He really did know what He was doing in creating couples. The Word says that Adam was alone; in other words, he was all one (al-lone). God said it was not good for him to be all one, or alone, so He made him a helper suitable for him. This is one of the purposes of marriage. We no longer are two individuals but take on a one flesh nature in every aspect. Together we accomplish the purposes of God. He no longer sees us as two individuals but as a singular unit. When God created Eve, He took a part of Adam from his rib, and put it into Eve. This leads to two points. First, while we support and teach biblical submission, it is important to remember God took a bone from Adam's side, not the bottom of his foot or even from his head. We therefore must remember to walk side by side as a couple to accomplish purpose. Secondly, after God created Eve, what was not found in Adam was now found in Eve, and what was not in Eve was still in Adam. This helps couples understand that we may not always do the same things or even have the same responsibilities. What it does mean is that as we are in agreement we will accomplish a common purpose for the kingdom as we support one another. Why? Because according to God's plan and perfect design part of what is needed is in him and part of it is in her. This is why the Word of God says:

> *Whoso findeth a wife findeth a good thing,*
> *and obtaineth favor of the Lord*
> *Proverbs 18:22*

When a man finds the rest of himself, in his God appointed mate, then he will be complete. When he is complete, and all of his pieces come together he will begin to see supernatural favor manifested in his life.

This is why it is important that we know the vision for our personal life. When we better understand ourselves, and know who has been purposed to "run" along side of us, and who has not we can better assess who will be a benefit and who will be a hindrance in our life. Remember the scripture in Habakkuk tells us to make sure we make our vision plan. In other words know it and understand it so that any prospects that come along can clearly see it, understand it and know for them self if they want to run with it or not.

Vision acts as an ark of safety for us. When we know the vision for our life, then it will act as a perimeter and margin to help keep us on the path to destiny, hopefully, keeping us from getting sidetracked by all of life's distractions.

> *Where there is no vision, the people perish...*
> *Proverbs 29:18*

There may be certain places we cannot go, certain things we cannot do, and certain people that we cannot connect with. Vision will help keep us from going outside the lines, perimeters, and boundaries of the road that leads us to our personal destiny.

In addition, Adam needed someone he could relate to. Thus, God created Eve for him. It is important to understand for those who desire companionship and to be married that God has someone exclusively designed just for you, someone suitable for you. It is equally as important that we prepare ourselves to not just get a spouse, but to be the best spouse that God has designed us to be.

Courting is a valuable tool for two reasons; it helps develop an inner connection as you learn about another person, and more about yourself. Also, courting will help an individual see how well they connect, or do not connect, with another individual *socially, intellectually, mentally, emotionally and spiritually.*

Through this process courting should tell you a whole lot about the other individual, as well as yourself. This is why courting should be taken serious, allowing different avenues that best represent you and your interests to be explored. Courting is different from dating because dating says lets go out, have a good time, and see what becomes of it. Too much is left to the wind and it is not driven by a commitment to discover God's best.

Few things could be worse than having someone who is absolutely miserable with you, or that you are absolutely miserable being with. The real key to developing intimacy comes more from communication than it ever will through sex. The word intimate comes from a Latin word meaning inner most. True intimacy is getting to know, or looking into, the inner most part of each other. As individuals we are spirit, soul, and body beings. True intimacy addresses two of these areas; it is the ability to be able to connect in the spirit and the soul (soul=heart, mind, will). This is unlike physical intimacy where the connection is merely in the flesh, or body. Couples, we have seen, that courted go into their marriage with an advantage that most, who only know physical intimacy, do not have. Couples who make this spirit and soul connection (intimacy) in courting only await sharing in the physical intimacy after marriage. For those who have experienced true intimacy, sex is simply a celebration and expression of that intimacy and love. As a couple shares the essence of who they are they reach a level that many never get to when they by pass the valuable courting process. However, those who experience only physical intimacy, prior to marriage, have a harder time developing true intimacy of connecting in their spirit and soul following marriage. For those who have not experienced true intimacy sex is the only level, of intimacy, they may ever experience. This undoubtedly can leave them vulnerable with a need to try and fill this inner most void with other people or other things somewhere down the line. Even after couples marry it is important to maintain the lines of communication; keeping them open so that intimacy continues to be fostered in the relationship. Once communication goes in a marriage generally all three areas of intimacy go as well.

Again courting is also a valuable tool that will help individuals see how well they connect in particular areas. Socially, it is important to know how a potential spouse handles himself or herself in a variety of settings and with different people. Are they introverted, extroverted, polite, rude, quiet, loud? Can they carry a conversation, or do they dominate every conversation? Do they have table manners, or act like their last meal was at the zoo? This helps ensure you have selected someone who is most compatible for you, and who best represents who you are. This is why in the courting process attention should be given to allow your self to see specific situations like how conflicts are settled, work situations are dealt with, etc. Don't just sit home, watch TV, go to the mall, and go eat all the time. Put yourself in a variety of situations so you get a good panoramic view of who the person really is.

Intellectually, we believe it is important to know what you are looking for. Some people prefer to have someone who has similar degrees of education or who has reached a certain attainment in their career. Others don't care. Either way regardless of the level of education and the type of job the person has, we suggest you give consideration to the person's degree of investment in self development and forward thinking, particularly about the future. Observe things like do they have goals? If so how will they reach them? Or are they satisfied with everything they have already done? This area is important because it helps gauge future interests and possibly direction.

Mental compatibility is equally important. This has to do more with the mental health, development, and the processing of mental faculties and is more in reference to mechanics than it is to content. Be aware of things like mood swings, depression, chemical imbalances, paranoia, and other issues that may need to addressed by a doctor. As well, look at family history. This area also involves how one processes information and comes up with solutions. Remember there are no right and wrong answers, but be true to your answers. What exactly do you want to deal with and what is best left alone? Often times a person's mental health is an indication of a much deeper rooted issue and gets expressed emotionally.

Getting to know someone *emotionally* is invaluable. Once again, through the process of courting, you begin to learn a person's temperament and disposition. This area is more important than people give credit to. Do not ignore this area, and do not ignore potential signs. Check and see if they are consistently moody, mean, rude, angry, happy, sad, verbally abusive, care free, serious, depressed, violent, controlling! Look at how they express themselves.

Or do they expect you to read between the lines? We know of a young lady who began dating someone from her church who always said things that were mean and hurtful and who was very controlling of her. While she was well aware of all his negative attributes, her heart was already involved and she banked on his better qualities as they discussed marriage just within months. Her family, friends, and even co-workers were very concerned about her, because she was just the opposite, a very loving and encouraging person. As it turned out he had deep rooted mother and authority issues which he was playing out with her. She did eventually sever the relationship. We shared all of this to say that this is why we suggest courting and not dating. Courting is a head-first process, not a heart process. Get the valuable information you need, make decisions based on the information, and don't ignore the red flags!

Knowing someone spiritually is vital to the short term and long term health of the relationship. We don't suggest that you become fruit inspectors, but definitely see if the two of you are in similar places with your relationship with God. Look at basic things like moral conduct, church involvement, their value on pastoral authority, tithing, and lifestyle.

When considering joining yourself with someone else, you can not only be concerned with the will of God for your own life, but you also have to be willing to understand, respect, and accept the will of God for the other person's life as well. Hopefully through courting you will begin to learn the will of God for the other person. Being unequally yoked can take place even among those who are in Christ. Therefore it is important to ensure your visions are compatible, but not necessarily identical. From here you will have to decide, with the wisdom of God, if it fits with your vision, purpose, and direction.

Courting is your opportunity to get and give valuable knowledge as you disclose and uncover needed information. At the end of the courting process you should be convinced that this is the one. On the other hand, if in courting you realize this is not it, be honest before either party continues to invest more valuable time, energy, and expectation.

ENGAGEMENT

The excitement of being in love and getting married just radiates from the bride-to-be, and those around her generally feel her excitement too. There's so much anticipation in the air of so much to do, so much to plan, and prepare for. Whether a year and a half, one year, or six months, it just seems like it's not enough time to do all that needs to be done for the special day. Bridesmaids have to be selected, and flowers, dresses, a cake, and reception hall to just name a few. In addition, colors for everything have to be selected and properly coordinated. At the same time an exotic honeymoon, china patterns, gift registry, guest lists, and drapes for the home all have to be finalized. It is almost like running a small business. It's no wonder weddings are a multi-million dollar industry with lots of money to be made.

Sadly enough, some brides spend more time preparing for the wedding day than they do preparing for the marriage. By all means, make preparations, and plan your wedding the way you want it done (within your budget), and have fun doing it. Just don't forget about the marriage. To focus 90% of your attention on the wedding and not the marriage is like Godiva Chocolates spending millions of dollars to design the candy wrapper and not put a dime into developing the flavor of their legendary chocolates.

The engagement is a very valuable time in the relationship. It has a two-fold purpose for the couple: it is a time to make preparations for the wedding, and it is a time to prepare to transition to becoming one.

By no means do we think couples should underestimate the importance of planning the actual wedding ceremony and celebrations because it is an important and sacred service. Remember the first miracle Jesus did was at a wedding where He turned water into wine.

The first reason the wedding is so important is because the couple is making a public confession of their willingness to be joined together with this other person to live out their life and fulfill purpose together. As a public confession, the wedding is a celebration of the continuance of the first institution given to us by God in Genesis, which is the family. In fact, we encourage couples that if you have found the one God has destined for your life, celebrate each other, your love, and commitment openly before others. It is not only the couple at the alter, but it is a three fold cord that includes God. Marriage is not a contract that can be broken at will, but it is a covenant between two individuals and God. Covenant is made between the three.

The wedding also gives those in attendance the opportunity to witness and agree to uphold the covenant that the two are agreeing to. Those in attendance who are witnessing the vows have a responsibility to encourage and uphold the covenant the couple is making between the two of them and God.

Marriage represents the ultimate relationship between Christ and his bride the Church. The wedding ceremony reminds us that our bridegroom, Christ, is returning for His bride, the Church, which is us. In anticipation of His return, we therefore must prepare and be ready. Often, many parts of the wedding ceremony are taken for granted as just being tradition or formality. However, they speak to the sanctity and covenant that God intended.

The second valuable purpose of the engagement period is to make practical preparations to become one. The engagement period is the time when the couple begins assessing their personal lives and obligations to determine how best to bring a second party into all of it. It is a valuable time because it should encourage and stretch individuals to really make sure that their personal affairs are in order. Practically speaking, every area should be looked at including health to finances, and from family to work, and from home to friends and acquaintances. No area should be overlooked. Make sure you have everything in order before bringing someone else into your situation. It is a lot easier on the two-becoming-one transition when things are already in place and you don't have to figure out the basic things as you go along.

The third valuable purpose of the engagement period is to make spiritual preparations for the couple to become one by getting necessary tools to sustain the marriage. This is where we encourage couples to not underestimate the premarital counseling. This is probably the most valuable tool available because we all come from different backgrounds, different families, and ultimately different ideals. This is a good way to ensure that you have the tools you will need, and that the person with you has the same tool bag as you. As turbulent times come you can be confident that the one you are with can help build your house with you and not tear it down.

Engagement is the time when couples are further equipped to have a successful marriage. Marriage is designed to be a reflection of Christ and the Church. Good marriages are not the result of a nice wedding ceremony, pretty flowers, or a lovely reception. Nonetheless, they are desirable to have and enhance the day for the couple and their guests. A good marriage is the result of two people's deliberate and intentional preparations and investments into their marriage, not just the wedding day.

CHAPTER 3

Pull Back The Covers
(Take Another Look At That)

Looking diligently lest any man fail of the
grace of God; lest any bitter root of bitterness
springing up trouble you, and thereby many be defiled:
Hebrews 12:15

Have you ever really thought about the story of Cinderella and all of the abuse, scorn, neglect, rejection, abandonment, and ridicule she faced at such an early age? Magically, all in one night she becomes the object of the prince's desire. He finds her, marries her, and they live happily ever after. That's the end of the story. Indeed this is a fairy tale. This is how we would love for our story to read. Unfortunately these are not the true life stories so often heard. We live in this thing called life and it happens to all of us. What the story doesn't talk about are her fears, insecurities, and the resulting issues of so much sadness and disappointment in her life. Even with the prince we don't know about his challenges of manhood, feelings of inadequacy, and trying to live up to high expectations. All we know is she looked great to him, and he married her.

However, it all makes you wonder would the Prince have still been interested in her if he knew her sad background. Would he still be interested if he knew she was the black sheep of the family? Would he have pursued her had she been in her usual dingy tattered clothes? Would he have thought twice if he knew she was basically the house servant? Would he have wanted her hearing how she was degraded by others? Would he have wanted to be bothered knowing she had issues of rejection, hurt, shame, and abandonment? Probably not! Without trying to defile a popular children's fairy tale, we submit that the Prince did not really know Cinderella. But then again Cinderella did not know the Prince. Was he a rich spoiled brat? Was he looking for a wife to pick up where his mother left off? Did he have father issues because his father was always away on diplomatic affairs? Or was he in rebellion of the lavish life he had lived? Again we submit to you that Cinderella really did not know the Prince, except that he was handsome and had the ability to take her away from a life of so much disappointment.

Why do we tell this fairy tale? Well because it is just that-a fairy tale. We want you to remember you are not in the story of Cinderella. I have always disagreed with the common cliché that "knowledge is power". I don't believe that. I believe, on the other hand, what you do with knowledge is what produces power. This I also believe is the practical definition for wisdom. We find the Cinderella/Prince factor happens so often in dating.

DATING

The deceitful thing about dating is we put our best foot forward. We want the other person to like us and see how wonderful we are. We want to display all of our good qualities. We want everything good about us to shine and stand out like a shiny new silver dollar. In a nutshell we want to be liked, and thought of in a Cinderella/Prince kind of way. As a woman we want the fairy tale of being swept off of our feet leaving all of the hurt, shame, and disappointment behind us. We want the validation of our self worth by being selected far above other women by the Prince. As a man we want to be the handsome prince who saves the beautiful Cinderella from all of life's ills. We want the validation of our self worth by being valued as a capable man above all other men. At the end of the day Cinderella and the Prince are not really that different. They both seek validation. They are looking for value to be assigned to them through the acceptance of another individual's love.

According to the story, they lived happily ever after. Although we know the story is not how things really happen, something in the back of our minds is still waiting for the right someone to notice us so we can live happily ever after. However, we submit to you who he got was not the reality of who she was, and who she got, well, she really didn't know a lot about him either. So what each got was probably not what they thought they had. Cinderella and the Prince both represented the *right* presentation, but not necessarily the *right* package.

Think about it, if you are putting your best foot forward and showing all your wonderfulness, all of you strengths and none of your weaknesses what do you think the other person is doing? If they hooked up with you the best guess is they are doing the same thing as you. Do you really think the other person is really Mr. or Miss Wonderful, have no weaknesses, flaws, struggles, problems or issues? Do you really believe their greatest weakness in life is being too sensitive and nice to others? Come on! You are really fooling yourself. Why would someone so perfect want someone like you with so many imperfections? The truth is that person is human just like you're human and is also living in their thing called life. If you don't understand this point, and go through life dating, you are positioning yourself to be taken advantage of and the very essence of your life will be sucked out of you. There is good, bad, and ugly in all of us.

One of the most unfortunate things about dating is that the other person rarely gets a chance to really know who you are. The other person may feel the same way about their self esteem and self concept issues that you do. We want to be liked and accepted; that's only natural since God has created us to be relational. The best way to go about this, dating tells us, is by only letting others see our good, and pile it on thick. If only they could see how wonderful I am. As a result of this, people often paint a picture they know is not true. In other words they present a lie about who they really are. Fears, disappointments, failures, mistakes, are often times seen as bad attributes but when we get healed from our past we can begin to see them as signs of perseverance, success, and our learning experiences.

Stress eventually in the relationship surfaces and becomes an issue when one tries to keep the idea of a perfect image alive about them self. The more the other person's affections grow, the more they grow for something that is not real. Right before their eyes, and in the heart of someone else, you are continuously transformed into someone who is not you, all to please someone who is ultimately not themselves either. More than a dating game, this sounds like a dating trap. After putting up a façade for so long, people begin to loose their identity, and forget their reality while putting themselves on display. Here I am, check me out while I show you what I think will be impressive to capture your attention and gain your acceptance.

Needless to say, this is very shallow, very surface, and generally does not last. Neither will it allow true intimacy to develop. It hinders the essence and basis of a true relationship which requires looking under the surface to see who a person really is. When the foundation of this relationship crumbles then the next suitor is pursued. This process inevitably continues like a merry-go-round--people getting off and people getting on as you continue to spin in the dizziness of relationship confusion.

COURTING

Some years ago I was asked to speak at a conference about the topic "Before you Date Investigate". When we first started working with couples, we used to think that one of the main problems they faced was with not knowing each other well enough. Today we don't see that as the primary problem. We now believe individuals do not know themselves well enough. Then secondly is the factor that people don't know the other individual well enough. For obvious reasons, this does not create a favorable environment for moving forward into a healthy relationship. Again, this is one reason why we highly recommend the courting process so a greater knowledge of self and the other person is fostered

In courting, we stress the importance of character versus personality. The object of dating, just discussed, is personality; the best foot forward. It stresses the outward appearance and what you see such as image, status, money and clothing. Often it's what we see and like in others that causes us to identify with something within us. However, the flip side of personality and image is that you may get used to further enhance someone else's image.

Character, on the other hand is in reference to who a person really is on the inside-whether good or bad. While outward and physical appearance is important, what's inside is of vital importance because it will always show up. While we need to take care and diligence in developing every aspect of our life, it is crucially important that we always continue to build our godly character within so that it is reflected on the outside. True character and integrity will not ask what you can do for me, but how can we bless and benefit each other.

We recently did premarital counseling for a young couple where the gentleman's story always stayed with me. He said he dated a popular young lady from his church who on the surface had great personality and every appearance of having it going on. He found himself having to dress a certain way, had to go to certain places, and had to be in certain company when he was with her. At first, he said, it was fun because it made him feel like he was in the in-crowd and it made him feel accepted. Eventually her requirements became a burden mentally, emotionally and financially. He realized that what she wanted of him was something other than who he was. When he wanted to do activities that he considered to be more along his nature, he was labeled a square. While she was beautiful on the outside, he began to see that on the inside they were two different people. When they broke up, he said it felt like a ton of bricks was lifted from his shoulders, and he never looked back.

Courting is a safe place and a safe way to get to know one another. One of the purposes of getting to know someone in courting is to determine suitableness and compatibility for marriage. Therefore courting is not the place to put your best foot forward, but to begin revealing who you really are. I believe it is always the intention to find out about the other person, but now the tables are turned and you must become vulnerable. You really have to be willing to show and share the truth of who you are. If who you really are is not what the other person is looking for, take a deep breath, thank God you found out sooner than later, and move on. Someone specific is out there that will value, respect and celebrate you for who God has designed you to be.

In revealing who we are to someone else, we often see things about our self that we did not necessarily know was there. This is not bad; this is a good thing if you are mature enough to deal with the person in the mirror. Don't just look at what you see and move on. Deal with your short comings and your issues in an honest way. Also, don't be so quick to be defensive. We are not saying that you have to accept and believe a lie, but make sure it's not the truth before you dismiss it.

One couple we did premarital counseling with was a perfect example of this. They were in the same church together for years before interest ever developed. They attended the same ministry training group and he said he could not stand to be in her group because she could always see right through him to his real issues. She was always able to get to the root. He couldn't stand it, yet he realized that she was always right. Because of this, he would always try to avoid being around her. It wasn't until years later that he began to realize that this was one of the attributes that he desired in a wife someone who stretched him with compassion to bring out the best in him.

A lot of who we are as adults is shaped by our family and our childhood. If you want to know where 90% of our issues come from in our adult lives, we guarantee you they are developed before we even turned ten years old. Much of what you see is just fruit from a much deeper root. Things like fear, rage, addictions are not the causes as much as they are the effects of something much deeper. In other words, because something happened early in life, these are the effects that resulted. Often times, these effects become part of our psyche which develop into our habits, idiosyncrasies, and sometimes strongholds. Things like abandonment, rejection, and shame have a powerful effect on us particularly during our developmental years. That is why we call it fruit. Fruit tells you what kind of tree is growing. I like to believe it is not who the person is as much as it is what the person exhibits. When you recognize what is at the root and deal with the root, then you can determine the kind of fruit you get. Remember, if you are not comfortable with yourself, then you cannot expect someone else to be comfortable with you either.

Remember, this goes both ways, with you and with the person you are involved with. Seed produces after its own kind. This is why it is so important that you take the time to investigate. One pastor says it this way and we find it to be so true, "what ever is not dealt with in one generation will be left to another generations to be dealt with". You want to get to know your prospective as much as you can, as well as what may be lingering on their family tree.

Several years ago we had a couple come to our office wanting to get married. We told them of our premarital counseling requirement and they decided that it was too long and too involved. They made a decision to go downtown to the justice of the peace. Because we personally knew the young lady and sensed issues with the gentleman just from the few encounters we had with him we advised that she not marry him. At the least, we suggested to her that she wait a little longer to get to know him better. Unfortunately, time told the story better than we could have. He never worked while he was with her, he abused drugs and alcohol, and there was domestic violence. His mother encouraged her to stick in there with him and for four years she did. However as things escalated and she feared for her life and her children's lives, she decided it was best to get out of the situation. Unfortunately she did go back into the relationship. While his issues are obvious, there were also issues in her life that caused her to connect, and reconnect, with someone she knew had serious issues.

There is an old cliché that says "fruit doesn't fall far from the tree". Courting is a great opportunity to find out about the tree that the fruit you are picking comes from. Does the word investigate mean anything to you? Finding out about their mother and father will prove to be invaluable information, particularly if you know what to do with it. Allow us to also warn against the savior complex which is when someone thinks they have to ride in on a white horse and save someone. Wrong! There is a root to that too. Jesus is the only Savior. Premarital counseling sessions are a great place to deal with all of these issues should you decide to move forward with engagement.

What's in your genes? Don't be fooled. Courting will help you see the value and potential in yourself and the other person, or it will help you see that this is not the one or not the time.

ENGAGEMENT

We have found that it is not enough to be in love. Rent and bills still have to be paid too. Neither is it enough to be equally yoked. When you leave church you still have to go home and live together. During courting you have discovered compatibility, and during the engagement and first years of marriage you will continue to learn even more about the other person.

If you have reached the point of engagement then you probably have also discovered that along with the compatibilities there are also several differences. These should be areas that compliment and/or do not take away from the relationship. Couples often find differences, like one person is talkative and the other is quiet. One may be a neat freak, and the other may be a little more tolerant of clutter. Engagement is the perfect time to discuss how to work with the differences. Don't get caught off guard when you return home from the honeymoon and life really begins. One cannot over estimate the power of planning. Likewise, it is a great time to continue to prepare yourself, and make sure personal areas are in place and in order before connecting with someone else.

We listened to Robin Givens be interviewed on the Oprah Winfrey Show and it was very sobering. She talked about how her mother told her that as she matured the things she did not think were sexy in a man would begin to change. Biceps and triceps start out looking great, but over time have the potential to change, like Popeye without his spinach. You might start out liking the red corvette he has, but the idea that he owns the house and garage it sits in begins to look more appealing than the car ever did. Things like a W-2, good FICO, balanced check book, up to date on bills, and being debt-free looks real attractive.

More stress is generally put on the man in reference to financial planning and preparing, and we agree that should be the case. Christ said in reference to his bride:

> *And if I go and prepare a place for you,*
> *I will come again, and receive you unto myself;*
> *that where I am, there ye may be also.*
> *John 14:3*

Therefore, we earnestly think it is the man's responsibility to have things ready and in place for his bride. We often remind couples that in the Garden of Eden, by the time Eve came into the picture, Adam was already working, had a home, and everything was in place and ready for Eve. He did not take her to his Father's house. If he did they both would have been dead because they would have been in heaven and not Eden. Adam had his own place.

Likewise, we like to encourage both parties to prepare themselves. We do not think it is a healthy idea for the woman to come with the perspective that she has to do nothing and that he will take care of everything. It still has to be a partnership. With a partnership both parties come to the table with something. We like to encourage couples to be prepared in several areas of their lives: Finances which includes credit, personal finances, and securities; also job, living situation, health, time management, and spiritual life.

Finances are one of the top three reasons for divorce because when finances are in disarray, it generally causes a great strain. This is especially one of those areas where both parties should be knowledgeable and should bring something to the table other than debt. We recommend the basics of at least a checking account to pay your bills, and a savings account to save for your future and emergencies. If you currently do not have either, get out of the habit of paying bills with cash and money orders and at the last minute.

Get in the habit of managing your finances, and have a good handle on them before you get married. Know what is coming in and know what is going out. It may sound silly, but have a system for even receiving your paycheck. Some people get paid, take their check to the bank, cash it, and by the middle of next week do not know where they spent their money! Direct deposit works best for many people when it can go directly into specific accounts without being spent first. Have a system for paying your bills.

A real biggy in the area of finances is the credit issue. We can't say enough about getting your credit together before you get married. In fact we almost encourage couples not to marry until this area is at least headed in the right direction. Order a copy of your credit report! Look it over and see what people are saying about your name. Are they saying you can be trusted, or are they saying that you cannot be trusted? How your previous creditors have labeled you will effect how future creditors will perceive you. How future creditors determine your name will effect how they determine your future credit and buying power. Clear up, fix up, and repair your credit. Start today. This needs to be a priority. Your credit will determine your ability to buy a house, car, furniture, vacation and so much more. Even if you are able to buy these things with bad credit it will cost you more because the interest rate for those with bad credit is always much higher. Higher payments obviously mean more money out of your pocket. Please whatever you do get this area together. Do it for yourself, your spouse, your future children, and just your life in general.

Also in the area of finances is what we call securities. This is the area that deals with benefits and insurance coverage. Make an inventory of what you are offered on you job and what you may need to take a second look at. Are you offered a 401 (k) or a 403 (b) plan, and perhaps is it something that your employer matches? Evaluate your retirement options and determine if you are taking the best advantage of what you are offered. Look at your insurance coverage and what you pay into it. Determine if it is meeting your needs, and look at if you are maximizing its use. You may need to speak with the Human Resource Manager on your job to answer some of these questions with you.

Often times young couples underestimate the need to look at life insurance. However there are two best times in your life to get life insurance. The first best time to get insurance is when you are still young. The earlier in your life you purchase insurance the lower your premiums will be. The second best time to purchase insurance is when you realize you do not have any insurance. As long as you are living it is never too late to get life insurance. Insurance takes us into our next point.

In terms of finances, we even encourage you, where and when possible, to have at least some type of investment so that you are not just living on a paycheck. Producing multiple streams of income will help you as your family grows not to live from paycheck to paycheck. This will help relieve some financial strain and burden. This may be a second job, but we caution against that if at all possible. Second jobs, particularly during that first year, have the potential of infringing upon the couples' time as you get to know one another, develop their lives, and grow together as a couple. However there are other options that people utilize such as rental income, consulting in your profession, selling off assets, money for hobbies, internet and so many more creative options are out there.

In reference to a job we encourage each party to be gainfully employed. Both parties need to start with a job and a work history. Often times people are already established in their career when they plan to get married; this is even better. It's a good practice for both to be able to refer back to several years of W-2's from one place of employment. This is a good factor, pointing to job stability. A work history that is sporadic and constantly changes is not a positive sign of possible future job stability. This may be something that can be rectified by further education or training. Evaluate your own situation and resolve it before marrying someone and bringing them into your situation. Unresolved, this can be a major point of stress on the relationship. If you are aware that you will be experiencing any major job transition, we encourage you to plan accordingly so the beginning of your marriage does not fall subject to volatile changes.

For example, we don't recommend engagement, or the first year of marriage, as the best time to start a new business. New businesses require an exorbitant amount of time investment and must be a major priority for success. During the first year of marriage, in particular, as you grow as one, the spouse, not a new business, should be the priority of time and investment. A new business may offer time conflicts while the couple is just getting established. What is done at the beginning of the marriage lays the framework for the years to come.

An individual's living situation is equally as important as their job situation. Make sure it is stable. Again try to make sure that you either have a history of mortgage payments or rent receipts for one address for no less than a year. Like a work history, frequent moving around is a sure sign of instability which again may cause unnecessary stress to a newly wed couple. We recommend, as much as possible, that parties have some history of living on their own, outside of their parent's home, for at least a year prior to marrying. This is particularly true for the man. Living on your own gives you the opportunity to learn the responsibility of taking care of your home and household. There is more involved than putting your dishes in the sink, keeping your laundry clean, and your bedroom door closed. The value of wise decision making is factored in as you have to decide between buying the new shoes and keeping the electric on. You have the responsibility of maintenance, expenses, utility payments, groceries, timely mortgage or rent payments, taxes, garbage expenses, and so much more. All of this for the first time, along with a new spouse, has the potential to be overwhelming. Whether couples share these responsibilities or one will handle the majority of them, we encourage both parties to at least know how to handle each aspect.

Make sure you are taking care of your health. The last thing that you want to do is to become a burden to someone where it could have been prevented. Eat right, exercise and get plenty of rest. In such a fast paced society, so much is rushed and on the go, but make your health a priority. Cut back on take out and eating out and prepare home cooked meals which will add to your life and the quality of your life. In terms of exercise there are many options that are available to you even if you do not want to join a gym. Take a walk, ride a bike, join a dance class, engage in your favorite sport with family or friends. Exercise is beneficial, and can be a recreational way of relaxing and unwinding after a long day at work.

Make sure you get plenty of rest don't try to be Wonder Boy or Super Girl. There are 24 hours in the day. Some are for sleep, some are for work, and some are for play. The balance of the three will help determine your quality of life. Or the imbalance of the three will help determine your stress level. Manage your time so that you get done what you need to do, but first determine what you really need to do. Often times we are doing far more than what we really need to do. List your top four priorities and structure your time around them.

Finally, last but not least, look at your spiritual life. Ask yourself the question "are you where you want to be in your relationship, walk, and lifestyle?" Determine if and how you can better develop this area if you decide it could use more developing. To keep this area in your life strong, we recommend that you have three types of people in your life a mentor, a brother, and a mentee. A mentor is someone who you deem to be more mature spiritually or at a different level that you aspire to. This is the person that you may go to for prayer or for spiritual questions and answers. Then you have the brother, which is not literally a brother nor a male, but is someone who is at your similar spiritual maturity level. This is generally a friend or may be someone you already fellowship with. Then there is the mentee. This is the person that you are able to pour into their life and encourage in Christ. This may be someone newly saved or someone struggling in an area that you have already successfully overcome. These relationships develop over time.

So again, love is not enough to get a marriage off to a good start, or to keep it happy. Marriage takes work. Engagement is a great time to begin the serious process of looking at oneself, the areas that comprise one's life, and how to best be a steward over it all. It's all a lifelong preparation, but what separates the ready from the not-so-ready couple starts before the couple ever walk down the aisle.

CHAPTER 4

Loves Me... Loves Me Not...
(Emotional Involvement and Romance)

I charge you, O ye daughters of Jerusalem...Do not
That ye stir not up, nor awaken my love, till he please.
Song of Solomon 3:5

DATING

The feelings and emotions of love and romance can go by many names. How about puppy love?!? How many times have we heard this said of a budding relationship? Or, even a crush? It sounds so cute and it appears to be so innocent, and it may be. However, it may also have the potential of permanently attaching another individual's heart and soul to your life who may end up not being a part of your life or your destiny

It is not unusual to hear about people later in life who have reconnected with their high school sweetheart. Because even after they graduated, went on with life, married, and had children their soul was still tied to their first true love.

Infatuation is about the excitement of the relationship, or the idea that he is tall, dark and handsome with hazel eyes. This involves rapid and intense feelings that quickly evolve. This happens too quickly to be emotionally healthy. This type of relationship is 99% heart and 1% head. The 1% head involvement probably asks the question "when will I see you again?" The problem with infatuation is that it is premature, emotion driven, and is not really love. The greater the intensity of infatuation, the greater the possibility of making irrational decisions about the relationship that will effect one's life choices such as decisions about sex, money, school, work, and other valued relationships. When infatuation is in the driver's seat, much of a person's life can be in jeopardy due to quick decisions that lead to a dead end relationship.

During dating relationships it is not uncommon for soul ties are developed. A soul tie is when one person's soul becomes intertwined to another individual's soul. Soul ties intertwine individuals through the three area of their soul: mind, heart and will.

The mind is our thinking mechanism and the place of rationalization, processing and our thoughts. Our heart represents our emotions and is the place that houses our feelings. Our will is the seat of our decisions and generates our choices. When a soul tie occurs, the soul takes on the other individual, often times unaware, with the duties, and responsibilities of marriage vows; for better or for worse…death do us part. Dating is too early to make this type of commitment with your heart, particularly when there is no commitment to sustain it. Even worse than this, is when the relationship dissolves and you are still attached to the other person. When you still intensely think about the person (mind), and feel a great deal for the person (heart), regardless if you like, hate, or love the individual you are no longer with. Your soul has been tied. This is generally when and where you recognize a soul tie has occurred.

When your soul is tied to another individual, outside of a marriage covenant, you rarely make choices that are best for you. This is whether you are still with the individual or you have moved on. This is why your soul being tied to another individual in marriage carries a different dynamic. In a marriage, in the spiritual real, the two individuals have legally, by heaven and earth, become one and are no longer two people. Because of the principles involved in marriage when an individual makes a decision that may be best for the other person it will also work for them because of the fact that they are no longer two, but one. This, the Bible describes as a mystery. We have seen where wives have not necessarily agreed with their husband, sometimes rightfully so, but when they submitted to their husband's ordained headship the situation at hand worked in her favor.

On the flip side we have seen our share of dating couples acting and living like they are married. They make married decisions that don't really seem to work for them. In the natural, the choices often seem logical and productive but because they are outside the sanctity and covenant of marriage, they get different results than what they planned for.

Emotional involvement in dating is equivalent to being at the right place, but at the wrong time. There is a lot to be said for this area. Far too often, feelings and emotions become the bedrock of where and why many relationship decisions are made.

As we look at the difference between romance, intimacy and sex we will see they are like fire and water. Not good or bad. They are gifts given to us by God when used within their proper context.

Man is a triune being; spirit, soul, and body. Dating attempts to satisfy each dimension of man's being without addressing each facet of him. This lends to the mirage of fulfillment in all three areas when in reality he is being depleted. In fact with each *encounter* individuals are left feeling even more displaced. This is because soul ties work both ways. Not only do you get a part of someone else, but you are leaving a part of yourself with someone else. With each new dating encounter individuals leave a part of their heart, mind, and will with someone else. Just like you are walking around with a part of someone else, someone else is walking around with a piece of you.

Intimacy, sex, and romance, really without thinking about each separately, may be perceived as synonymous, but are not. Each is biblically identified and intended to satisfy a specific part of our humanity. Used out of context, without properly discerning their potency, individuals will be left with such issues as soul ties, fragmentation and brokenness. However, within the proper context, God designed marriage, their potency is exponentially greater.

Relationship is the real desire of man. The essence of relationship is intimacy. But as discussed earlier, dating is not designed to achieve this goal.

In dating intimacy has most closely been associated with sex. In fact they are sometimes used interchangeably. This, however, is in fact not the basis of true intimacy at all. *Real intimacy can lead to sex, but sex does not lead to real intimacy.* Intimacy is something that is developed over time, not over a martini or a coffee. Intimacy also involves risk whereas one has to risk personal vulnerability and exposure. Intimacy involves a deep sharing of the inner most part of who we are, what we are, what we desire, who we will become.

Romance on the other hand, during dating, is more closely associated with the intoxication of infatuation from the excitement of the relationship. Romance is basically the feeling that we get from being desired and wooed, thus fulfilling something within whether it is the excitement of the chase or being chased, pursuing or being pursued, and everything that entails. It's what gets the adrenaline pumping, and all the other hormones along with it. It's the turn on, and it's exciting. How many times have we seen when the romance is gone, the fun is gone, and excitement is gone the relationship too is gone. In dating, romance is often times the cornerstone of relationships, to the extent that the relationship hinges on romance or the lack of it. Too many times when individuals' are no longer excited, or turned on any more, they also decide they are not interested anymore. When it all becomes boring and dull, it also becomes time to move on to the next excitement. It's on to the next one, the next chase, and the next pretty face. This goes both ways. It's not just the men, it's the women as well. It's not a gender issue; it is a heart issue.

Romance is the desire of the soul. Think about it. Our soul is our heart (emotions); intellect (mind); and will (my choices). I always say "Willy" is a bad boy. Romance tickles every part of the soul. The soul's desire is romance.

Flirting is the first cousin of romance. Adrenaline tests how far you can go and still be safe. And all the other hormones are edging it on.

Sex, well, is just that, it's sex in the dating game. The dangerous part of sex is that it connects, attaches, and ties the souls of two individuals more intently, exponentially quicker, longer and tighter. There doesn't need to be any connection except for physical attraction, and we see and hear so often from song lyrics that that does not even need to be a factor. Sex does not even require a pretty face, just a willingness to go all the way.

The problem with sex before marriage is you are giving away a part of yourself that the laws and principals of God have determined there can be no exchange for. In other words because you are giving something away outside of marriage that God has intended to only be given away inside the covenant, of marriage you do not get the benefits of its equal exchange. It's just given away. It's like if I stole a pair of jeans from the department store, no matter how much I like them, or how much I think they are mine, and how good they look on me because the censor is still attached, I cannot enjoy having it. The excitement of boosting them and trying them on at home is nice, but I can not enjoy possession or ownership, because they are not mine. This is good place to caution you about secret relationships. If you cannot tell your pastor, you only meet in private and cannot go out in public together—beware.

What's more, is you begin to feel empty and unfulfilled because someone who is not one with you now has a part of you. Because you are operating outside the principals and laws of God, it makes it difficult to reclaim your fragmented pieces. Like the other gifts given to us by God, sex has been designed by Him to bring fulfillment to us. The difference is sex before marriage takes from us, whereas sex after marriage is intended to be a benefit to us. Outside of their God designed context sex is selfish and for self gratification. Sex becomes the ultimate deception of dating because it falsely interpreted says "I love you" to a lonely heart. This is why it is not difficult to convince someone "if you love me, than you will…", because they too believe they are having a void filled and met.

Often people do things out of habit, tradition, or ignorance with good intentions, but without really realizing what they are getting themselves into. Often times, principals are being set in motion over our lives-sometimes good and sometimes not so good. To truly have all of what God desires for us, we must be determined to do it the way God has designed it to be done. We have to seek the wisdom of God and not the traditions of man to get God results.

It is often said of men, all they want is one thing. This one thing is generally understood to be sex. Men, however want the same thing women want. They want companionship, intimacy and connection. Men like love, romance and intimacy like women like love romance and intimacy. To think less is to not understand men. Women enjoy sex just as men enjoy sex. Again, to think anything less is not to understand women. But more than not understanding men or women, I would say it is an issue of not understanding God. This is how God has created and designed each of us with the capacity to give, receive, and enjoy all these areas, but under the right circumstances. They have been created for us and for our enjoyment. They are to be a blessing to us. What may be different in men and women is their expression of what they like and how they like it

Dating is too premature to have emotional involvement and romance. A lot of times in dating we just dive right in and start telling people about the person we just met; we don't know them for two weeks or two months and already we love them and they know all about our life history. They know too much. And I love you is too much.

I think we can all agree that it is just too premature, especially when you do not know that this is your life partner. The picture to look at is this: if I am romancing you and whatever that leads to if you are not the one I just romanced somebody else's spouse. That is what that boils down to. In the Body of Christ we have to be more careful about that. I understand we are doing the group fellowship. On our wedding day our spouses need to be able to only see us and not our string of experiences and potential emotional attachments behind us. He doesn't need to contend with all of my thoughts about Harry, Billy, and Joe, and the comparisons whether we were physical or not. In modern dating, there is too much investing of our emotions, it is inappropriate, and this is not the time or place for it.

COURTING

Courting is still not the time or place to introduce strong emotional involvement, but to make the other party aware of your intentions. This includes your honest intentions for the relationship as far as who you are and the goals and direction for your life. If the truth be told, if more people utilized the courting process, they would be able to say this is the true incubation stage for true intimacy. The components of real love and intimacy are not microwave or magic, they come through a process of getting to know the *within* of an individual. This is the dimension of the relationship where you begin to know someone through open and honest dialogue and relating. Here is where you really begin to learn intimacy is most closely related to the head than it is to the heart.

During this process, both individuals really need to be able to think with their head and not just their heart to make sure that their life choice is the right choice. This stage is about assessing "is this person the one". Once the heart is involved and you begin thinking with your heart and not your head, a lot of relevant and crucial information gets past you. We hear it far too often in marriage counseling "I didn't know", "I thought s/he would change", "I thought our love would change it" "I didn't think it was a big deal".

Utilize this time to find out where the other person's head is as well as where their heart is. Find out how they handle situations, family, finances, crises, how they communicate, what their values are. What are they passionate about? Do they have educational plans down the road? Do they plan to relocate or change careers? Do they pay their bills, and are they on time? Do they own anything-car, house, or just debt? In what direction is God leading them? Is that the same direction you feel like you are going? Believe me it makes a big difference.

We don't believe that there are right or wrong answers, but you have to make sure they are the right answers for you. If you notice a red flag that pops up, don't just ignore it. If you cloud out all of the critical information with feelings of being in love, then chances are it will come up again. Our experience with couples tells us it always shows up after "I do". Sometimes it shows up in not feeling fulfilled, stress, sickness, over working, affairs, discord, you name it.

A couple come into our office for premarital pastoral counseling who already had a wedding date and many of their arrangements were already planned. Because they both had their own apartments the question about where they would live came up in the midst of their counseling. They were both on the same page about buying a home. However, their values that determined where they would buy a home were on two different pages. It eventually came out that because of the value he put on his family relationships, he desired to live close to his family. While she loved and respected her in-laws-to-be, she had no desire to live in close proximity to his family, or even her own. Neither of them were right, and neither of them were wrong. They were on a different page in regards to something that was important to them. They had different values that they felt strong about that went deeper than the geographical location of a home. This is the point where they rethought their decision to marry. The unfortunate part of this was all of the time, emotions, and finances that were invested into the relationship. The good part of this was the issues came out and were discussed before they said "I do".

Who was right and who was wrong? We believe both were right. They knew what they wanted and what they did not want and decided that maybe marriage was not the best decision for them. They were not on the same page about underlying issue, neither did they think they would be.

Fortunately enough for them, invitations had not gone out, but deposits had been placed on the hall, catering, etc. For them, they were already in the engagement process without first completing all the necessary aspects of courting. Courting helps assess the compatibility in a way that emotional involvement doesn't reveal. Our thoughts are they were very mature individuals to be able to assess their needs, values and concerns and rethink the wedding.

The results of getting to know each other are well worth the courting process. The results are experienced even during engagement. The intimacy of getting to know one another helps to build a powerful team and accomplish oneness as the couple move forward into marriage preparations. Together, they are more likely to achieve, what God has united them for.

ENGAGEMENT

For where your treasure is, there will your heart be also.
Matthew 6:21

The engagement stage signifies that everything is a go ahead moving ahead toward marriage with definite plans underway. While you are preparing for marriage, remember you are not yet married. While it may be a sure go ahead remember to respect yourself and your integrity before God, your parents, and others by not allowing the enemy to convince you that you are as good as already married. A more intimate friendship is characterized here. However what would still be considered inappropriate are things like sexual conversation, personal touching and petting. Expressions of feelings becomes okay within boundaries. However in this chapter engagement is discussed in light of making preparations towards the other individual. This is where the challenge of *me* versus *we* starts and really begins to be realized. Steps toward this new relationship are being prepared for during engagement by looking at more personal concerns of personal belongings.

We do not recommend, by any means, that you sign your fiancé onto you personal assets at this stage prior to marriage. The only one exception to this rule, we think it may prove to be a good idea to have one joint account, when both parties save money for the purpose of wedding expenses. If only one person is paying for the wedding, then this probably won't need to be done. Nonetheless, begin to think about, and include making preparations for after the wedding to bring your future spouse into your life in the in the areas of: finances, property and insurance. This area is probably the one aspect where we hear a lot of sad stories.

We often think about one couple who happily married and two weeks later the husband had a heart attack and died. For this new bride, this was a double whammy because he had not gotten around to changing any of his information, particularly adding his wife to his insurance policies. Needless to say, in the middle of her grief she had to find out that everything was left to other family members and she ended up with nothing. The church ended up financially supporting her for some time after this.

If you have not already done so, make the person aware of what you currently have in place. In regards to finances, make sure that you have discussed who, and how finances, will be handled in your home. Discuss what banks or credit unions will be best for you as a couple based on your needs. As well as what type of accounts will meet your needs as a newly wed couple just starting out together. We personally recommend combining resources to prevent a spirit of "this is mine and that's yours". In fact we found two principals to be true: where your treasure there your heart is, and when to people walk in agreement there resources go further. We always recommend a savings account where you plan and save together. But you may also want to have a checking account that your bills are paid out of. Again try to avoid *my* bills and *your* bills. Make each person's bills both person's responsibility and priority. Something optional, that we see some couples do, is have a separate expense account where the couple decides on personal budgets to buy miscellaneous and incidentals they want or need.

Also under the topic of finances create a plan to save. When savings are available, it helps emergencies not be crises whenever they occur. Together, discuss what your goals are, and what the two of you think would be comfortable to save. Together, agree upon what type of emergencies warrant you to go into your savings. This may need to be readjusted after you get married, but at least it is on the table and you have a starting point.

Don't forget to plan how you will set your budget. One valuable piece of information is to not live at your means, and definitely not above your means. Different couples have different goals, concerns, and lifestyles and therefore must evaluate what is important to them and their lifestyle. This may mean that you will have to decide as a couple where you want to fall between the spectrum of financial security and financial status. This will determine how you budget and conduct your finances. Whatever you do, make sure you plan and make sure you are in agreement about the plan.

A different type of story along the same lines is with a couple we know where the wife owned the home prior to them getting married. For whatever reasons, they never took the time to put the husband on the deed after they were married. The wife reminds and reinforces her independence through the home she owns where the family lives while they keep their finances separate; his and hers. They both work and have good jobs, but whenever a point of contention arises she is quick to remind him that he is living in her home.

Obviously this is not a good scenario. Again we stress after the marriage the two become one in all areas. If you have reservations and/or trust issues with the person you are marrying than most likely it's not the deed that needs to be rethought, but probably the marriage.

How you will handle personal property needs to be discussed prior to marriage because chances are this will be a little more lengthy process than just adding someone's name to a bank account. You will probably have to speak with your lawyer and maybe even your accountant or other financial advisor to have the necessary paperwork drawn up and find out the best ways to go about this process.

Finally insurance is another area where pre-preparations need to be made. There is both the issue of health insurance and life insurance. Many jobs today offer health insurance. As a couple you may want to sit down, compare plans, and again discuss your needs and family planning to see what is the best coverage for you as a couple. In regards to life insurance, we recommend particularly to the man, that this be one of the areas that has already been taken care of prior to marriage. Make sure you have insurance! And make sure you have adequate coverage based on your income, family, etc. A good insurance agent will cover all of these basics with you. Nonetheless, make preparations before you get married to make your spouse as your beneficiary. Gather your paperwork, contact your carrier, and set an appointment before your wedding date or honeymoon to get this taken care of after the wedding.

Investments, inheritances, and filing taxes, and financial responsibility of previous children are other areas that you will want to discuss and determine how they will be factored into marriage. Whatever you do make sure you are on the same page before you say "I do".

CHAPTER 5

Say What!

(Accountability)

Submitting yourselves one to another in the fear of God..
Ephesians 5:21

Where no counsel is, the people fall:
but in the multitude of counselors there is safety.
Proverbs 11:14

DATING

One of the primary reasons we don't recommend dating is because of the two words Webster's Dictionary offers for the word accountable. They are *responsible* and *answerable*.

As you really begin to look at dating and the dating process you quickly begin to see that many aspects of it don't go far beyond what looks good and feels right. In dating, the only person you are really accountable to is yourself. What feels right, what looks right, and what sounds right are all translated into what I think is right for now. However not realizing that flesh and hormones are steering the Love Boat, that you are riding, often transform it into the Titanic while you are still on board. Instead of an island oasis you find yourself headed straight toward an iceberg.

Often as youth, we don't have the forward capacity of calculating in *all* of the other *others* of life past who I am today, where I am today, what I want today verses who I will be tomorrow, where I will want be tomorrow, and what I will want for my life tomorrow. Even as adults, we sometimes forget to reevaluate, redirect and reposition ourselves to really attract the type of person that is desired for a current life and lifestyle. In our experience, we have often found those most successful relationships generally factor in the type of person that fits into their future "I wants" in contrast with those who factor their "I wants" around a particular person. Mr. or Miss Yesterday with today's goal realizations may not always still be compatible. So we have to look at not just who can be a part of all that has been accomplished, but someone who with similar accomplishments sees the necessity of together maintaining and sustaining what has been accomplished. For the most part, dating doesn't really do this. This is a process of the mind and particularly, the will. The focus of dating, however, is on the heart enjoying today's moment.

When courting evolved into dating and left the young ladies homes, much more left with it. Accountability also left and was taken out of the hands of parents and went to the social mores of the time. As society continued to change, the morals continued to change, and eventually accountability was left to peer groups and individuals. In dating accountability, from what we can see is pretty much thrown to the wind. For the most part it is viewed as nobody's business but my own. Except for peer groups involved, much of dating is done behind closed doors and in secret.

Because of this it is easier to be more sexually involved with less attachments. When things no longer look or sound right than each party has an easy button to get out quick. The Bible refers to this as every man did what was right in his own sight. The world calls this every man for himself, or the survival of the fittest. We may hear it dressed up as "we decided to see other people", " she/he wasn't my type", or "it just didn't work". More than often, though, somebody is already seeing someone else.

Unfortunately, particularly for youth who are still developing emotionally and mentally this often leaves them crushed and devastated with waning hope for their tomorrow. This has been a major contributor to what has been named one of the major causes of teen suicide. It's hard for some to digest the idea that he just doesn't want me anymore, or she just doesn't like me anymore. For some, it is difficult to their whole life ahead of them, and that this too will pass.

COURTING

Unlike dating, those who are courting have several avenues of accountability. We have found the main reason for this is because they are a little more seriously in marriage selection opposed to just enjoying the moment. In dating the idea of someone looking over your shoulder may be considered intrusive and nosey. Remembering that the objective of a courtship is not just to go out and have a good time, but is for those who are preparing for marriage selection. Therefore, individuals who are courting allow themselves to be open to other's constructive input pertaining to the goals of the relationship.

Remember from dating just a few paragraphs earlier we said accountability is being responsible and being answerable. One area of accountability that is often overlooked is among the two individuals involved. This is probably the most basic level of accountability. In healthy relationships the individuals involved are willing to listen and respond to the other and recognize the relationship is not just about one person. Therefore each person in the relationship must display responsible actions whereby the other individual is able to count on their level of maturity. This is how basic respect is established and built. Without these basic foundations, the bedrock of any relationship is unstable causing cracks in the foundation making it more susceptible to further eruptions and quakes.

Even more than mutual accountability courting recommends a third party for accountability. Next to the Holy Spirit, this is one of those factors that will help keep you. Someone other than the two individuals involved in the relationship is always a good idea.

Consider a neutral third party who has both individual's best interests in mind. This should be a person who will help you stay focused with your relationship and your life as a result of the relationship. This is someone who is able to help you see yourself and direct you in areas uncertainty. It should also be someone strong and mature enough to help guide you back in the right direction if you go off in the wrong direction. Remember, courting is not just about looking at the other person but also looking at your self. We encourage couples to identify someone who will respectfully get into your business and up in your stuff, someone who is honest and real with you, someone you are honest and real with, someone you do not mind telling your struggles to, knowing you will not be judged but supported and directed. Identify someone who can see through your lie, but someone who will not lie to you about what they see in you, or what they see you doing.

Among those that best qualify to be considered are parents, godly leadership, and other couples with proven marriages. Allow the person or couple to be someone with similar values, and to be someone who is where you desire to be spiritually and in your relationship. We do not recommend peer relationships many times, unless it is someone strong enough to tell you when you're wrong, while at the same time pointing you in the right direction.

When people come to us, we don't just let them come and not ask them certain questions. Of course we are going to ask certain questions. The goal is that your relationship, potentially your marriage, be blessed. A couple who came in some time ago were honest, "we live together Reverend and we do some stuff". I said "you guys are coming to a Pastor because you want me to help you prepare for marriage and bless your marriage. I can't bless what God is against. I don't mind marrying you if you go through the process. But the day of your wedding, I want to be able to bless it, so I have an assignment for you. No more sleeping together until you are married." Upon seeing them again they were asked "how are you doing?" He said "oh my God I'm, struggling. I knew not to come in. I knew I was going to be asked-yeah we messed up." The man said he didn't have a problem until he was told not to. It was explained again that our position is not to judge or condemn, but prepare, help, and bless. We're glad he was honest and told the truth so he could get more tools, go forward, and be steadfast.

ENGAGEMENT

Therefore shall a man leave his father
and his mother, and cleave unto his wife:
and they shall be one flesh.
Genesis 2:24

While marriage is a blessing, the Word of God also says it is a mystery. Taking two flesh people and making them into one flesh is really more than a notion. I know we envision the beautiful flowers, white dress, ten tier cake and the honeymoon night. Nonetheless, all of that is just one day in a lifetime. There needs to be ample preparation for when the honeymoon is over. The couple needs to be able to assess their checklist of things accomplished during this time and get necessary tools to live together as husband and wife.

When one reaches the stage of engagement, the number of those that he or she becomes accountable to increases. Where there may have only been one at the point of the engagement, several others are included in the preparation process. Prior to setting a wedding date the premarital counselor is further invited into the process. In addition, the individuals become even more accountable one to another as the commitment level has risen marriage consideration to marriage selection.

At this stage in the process both finance and fiancée make sure each other is vigilantly progressing and preparing as time moves toward the marriage. It will be a matter of time before both are able to assess the value of their proper preparation.

It's good during this process to be aware of where the other individual is pertaining to their challenges and successes. In other words, deliberately be aware of what areas you are working on and what areas the other person is working on. Some may be areas that you can assist with, but for the most part they are the responsibility of each individual. If one party does not hold up his or her side of the bargain, so to speak, the other party needs to assess either postponing the date or if they will move forward with unmet obligations. This is important because unmet obligations have grave potential of causing problems down the road. One spouse may feel they adequately invested in preparing but did not get the same respect of the other person doing the same, or following through with their pre-marriage commitments. This can be damaging if one feels they are not getting out of the relationship the same as they are putting into the relationship. Therefore, in review, make sure you personally address the following areas of finances, job, housing, health, education, time management, and spiritual life in your life and your future spouse before moving forward:.

A young couple we know was preparing to be married and the young man decided to quit school during his last year. For her, that was not a part of their plan. She told him that he would not be able to offer her all that they had discussed and decided that she would not move forward into marriage. The young man rethought his plans and finished school and they were married. This may sound harsh to some but to her it was already a red flag about his commitment to follow through, and his ability to be able to provide for her in the future.

We recommend that before setting the actual wedding date the couple first schedule an appointment to meet with their pastor or whoever will be involved in their pre-marital counseling. This is important because the pastor may see areas that may need more time and/or development than what the wedding date will allow. We often see with couples who already have dates that they predicate the counseling around the date, instead of the date around the counseling. When couples properly plan and commit to the process they can generally complete the premarital pastoral counseling within the time of their projected date.

We greatly recommend the couple go in open minded and ready to hear, and not look at the premarital counseling as a prerequisite. Over the years, we have seen all kinds of scenarios. The worse of which is when people come in only as a formality. They know there are issues that need to be addressed, and really don't want counsel, they just want to say I came. At our church, while premarital pastoral care counseling is strongly encouraged, we can always tell the difference between the couples who come because they *want* to come from those couples who come because they feel like they *have to* come.

The truth is we get into all of the couple's business that we recognize has the potential to affect you and the other person's life. We address everything from your parents, previous relationships, health, childhood, finances, and more. Not because we just want to know their business. Our job is to make sure that when they do tie the knot it does not become unraveled by life, lies, or forgotten information. The other person has a *right* to know about everything they are getting into. We had one couple come in for counseling and the man revealed everything but the fact that he had another child. Eight months into the marriage the other lady decided that she would start requiring child support. Sure enough they started garnishing his wages. What a way for the wife to find out. Her words have always stuck with us. "I had a right to know, so I could decide if I still wanted to go through with it" she said. When you find things out like that it makes you wonder what other secrets are lurking in the dark.

Life does not generally show up on the wedding day or the wedding night, but rest assure life does show up. What better time to get the tools than before you need them. It would be foolish to begin building a house without a blueprint, hammer, nails and a saw.

Because we recognize that marriage is ordained by God, is sacred, and should not be entered into unadvisedly our personal stand is that we will not unite a couple in Holy Matrimony if they have not submitted first to the premarital counseling process. We have had several couples go to the justice of the peace and make different arrangements because the process became uncomfortable, or deemed to be to involved or too long. We had one young lady tell us "who has time for all that". We don't think it is fair to them, or fair to God, to sanction a covenant that we have not done our part to prepare them for, ultimately prepared them to keep. What kind of parent would we be if we just handed our car keys over to our children knowing they have not had any drivers education? They become a hazard and a threat to both themselves and those around them. In addition to this, we are accountable to God. We believe if we assist someone in entering marriage unadvisedly we have to stand before God should their vehicle wreck. Needless to say we have had couples come to us only to get married, but did not want counseling. But after hearing our position some have preferred to go to City Hall and stand before a judge because they wanted to get married now!

My husband use to tell people when they came to us "my job is to get you to change your mind". Not really, but what he was saying is we are going to go over this relationship with a fine tooth comb so that you are certain, beyond a shadow of a doubt, about what you are doing, what you are getting yourself into, that you're sure you really want to do this, and that you have the necessary tools to build and sustain it.

Again one of the purposes of engagement is to prepare for both the wedding and the marriage. We cannot guarantee you will not have any difficult times, but we can definitely tell you that you will be more prepared to deal with whatever challenges you face. Over the years we have had couples who have changed their minds about getting married, and some who have postponed dates because they felt they were not ready. However, we have also had many couples back and tell us they have had to use the tools and they worked.

CHAPTER 6

Looking For A Well
(The Parents Part)

Children, obey your parents in the Lord: for this is right.
Honor thy father and mother; which is the first
commandment with promise; That it may be well with
thee, and thou mayest live long on the earth.
Ephesians 6:1-3

DATING

Parental exclusion has become pretty much the norm. Many parents recognizing their child is with someone who is not right for them don't feel they have an ear to give wise counsel. In fact peer influence and opinion is often times valued higher than that of a parent.

Because modern dating is mostly going out, thus primarily away from the home, very little to no parental involvement is typical. In fact the general thought is I don't need their involvement; I can do this on my own. Most people would find it unthinkable that when they find someone they are interested in to ask their mother or father for their opinion. In fact many parents do not meet the significant other until their child brings them home to say "this is it, this is the one". We live in a time where you hear people justify their relationships by using "God told me he's the one", "God said I'm suppose to marry her", "God showed me…". However I love how many parents, when involved, can discern a yes or a no and cut right through all of that.

Today, dating removes youth and young adults from the authority of parental oversight, counsel and concern. Cyber dating, my space, face book and other cyber social sites make this increasingly possible. In fact many cut parental involvement right out of the equation, leaving major decisions in the hands of minors. It's a dangerous thing.

Parents are not just another somebody in our lives, they are who God has ordained for our lives. Their role is so crucial to the life and success of marriage. This is seen more outside of the United States in other countries and cultures. The interesting part, that many loose sight of is that it doesn't even matter if they are saved or not or if they are "honorable" or not. God has purposed that we honor their position. Why? That it will go well with us. This is probably one principal that many struggle with particularly if the parents are absent, not saved, or not honorable. It's the position, more than it is the person. The blessing is in the position-or office-that they hold as parents in our life. Those who have issues with authority may particularly be challenged here, and more than likely roots back to parental issues.

Those areas that we have not respected our parents, or have made judgments against them are the same areas we can expect we will be faced with challenges in our own marriage.

Another important point worth mentioning as a side bar is that some of us as parents need to begin honoring our own parents so our children have an example to follow. If our children see that we do not honor our own parents they have no *example* to honor us. They have no *motivation* to honor us. We need to not only honor our parents, but we most also deliberately allow our children to see us honoring our parents so it becomes the prototype of the Kingdom of God to them. This way they will know how they are to treat us when they are up in age. It's not a principal that is just for little children in Sunday School, it is for everybody. God never says anything about our saved parents, or even our honorable parents. He just says to honor your parents-both of them!

COURTING

Whoso findeth a wife findeth a good thing, and
obtaineth favor of the Lord.
Proverbs 18:22

Understand the dynamics of selection. Just because you are selecting doesn't necessarily mean you will be selected. And, vice versa. Technically, selection is a two way street and for there to be a relationship vehicles must go both ways.

The idea of parental involvement in courting is rooted in the fact that a parent knows their child, beyond the surface. That knowledge assists them in the development *of* spousal selection and development *for* spousal selection. Ideally speaking, this has already taken place the duration of the person's life, and is an ongoing process leading to this point. When life, and the course of time, up the ante through a developing relationship parental involvement further assists one in choosing and being chosen. Thus the twofold process:

preparing to select a life spouse and being prepared to be selected as someone's spouse.

The first part of choosing has more to do with the process of critical thinking. You must ask critical questions, particularly of yourself. To thy own self be true about what you really want and what you do not want, what you are willing and unwilling to do, put up with, commit to, compromise, etc. We personally know of several bachelors and bachelorettes we think would be the catch of anyone's day—they meet the profile. However, we have to admire their truthfulness with themselves. Many are in a place in their life where they might like the occasional companionship but when they weigh it out, they do not want the real responsibility of being a husband or a wife. This is why we recommend a hold on emotional involvement so you can cognitively process what all of this means for you. On a different note we know of several people who knew they did not want the responsibility of being a husband or wife. However, because they were emotionally involved, or a baby was factored in they made a decision for something deep down they really did not want. They ended up telling themselves they had to do the right thing.

Far too many times this is where couples drop the ball. They see warning signs and things that aren't quite right but they have already been bit by the love bug. Now that they have love fever they have become delusional tossing out their better wits. People make decisions they would have never made had they not had love fever. One thing we have found about pre- and post marital issues is chances are if it is there before you marry, not only will it be there after you marry, but it will end up being a bigger issue than before.

Individuals really need to evaluate if they just want to be married or do they want to be a husband or wife. Likewise, are they just looking for someone to get married to, or are they looking for a husband/wife. Don't just get hooked up, men get your self a real wife. Women, get your self a real husband. But remember, you cannot ask for what you are not willing to do, or to be, to someone else. This leads to the next point of being chosen.

Being chosen has something to do with a little word we do not hear too often today particularly in the western societies. Dowry! To many people it sounds like an antiquated concept, but surprisingly enough, it is still very much alive in many cultures. A dowry represents two things: having something to offer and it represents an individual's value they bring to the marriage. One of the most interesting things about dowry is it involves the families, not just the couple.

We actually know a young man from India where his dowry price has already been set based on his worth and potential as a husband. Taking into consideration his education, accomplishments, family background, etc. Another young lady we know from Africa, although marrying an American, her dowry too is based on her worth and potential as a wife taking into consideration her education, background and accomplishments.

The concept behind dowry is not about buying an individual, or exchanging an individual for monetary value. The concept behind dowry is that the son, or daughter, is of great value to their family because of the many sacrifices and great investments that have been made into his or her life. The dowry represents an acknowledgement by all parties, potential spouses and their families, that this person, like a precious gem, has been reared and invested into, and is of great value and worth and will not just be given away to just anyone. In particular to someone who will not discern their worth and be able to support and maintain their value. Therefore the parents are not just giving this child away without recognizing that their child is of great value and worth.

While culturally speaking, we do not pay a monetary dowry, what we bring to the table should be the worthy equivalent in the sense of having something to offer the relationship. This is both symbolic and meaningful in several ways and demonstrates the idea that you must be prepared and able to offer something that will contribute to the relationship. Parental involvement is important because parents often have a keen understanding of their children's potential and worth and know what will add to them or subtract from them. This all translates into having a platform and a package-not baggage.

Your platform is about what you have to stand on. This, we like to believe, is the obvious what you bring to the table in terms of a job; what will pay the rent, buy food, diapers, and all of that. Your package is about who you are and what's in you in terms of your character, commitment, aspirations, and how you carry yourself.

What about you? What do you have to offer? Financially? A work ethic? A good name? A pure heart, body and mind? Temperament? What about homemaking skills, commitment and service to God at a local church? Make sure what you get is more than measurements or biceps. Likewise make sure what you have to offer is more than measurements or biceps.

The tricky thing about all this dowry stuff, particularly the package, is you have to invest the necessary time to make sure you don't end up with a good looking knock off imitation. Use the built in help God has given. Courting is the process we go through that will give us a little additional help when, and where we need it. This help comes through people who know and love us.

It's amazing for us to look at our two different children. At least by the age of five we could see what type of spouse each of them will need, and which type of spouse will not work for each of them. We fully understand they will continue to grow up and develop even further into who they are. However, just the personalities that God has given them says some definite things about them as individuals and what type of individuals have the ability to partner with them in fulfilling their purpose. Further as parents we know the time, tears, sacrifices and finances that we have invested into our children to be who God has purposed them to be. We are not willing to just hand all this over to someone who cannot, or does not, discern their worth.

This is why it is so important that we allow parents into our process, because they really do want the best for you-they've invested a lot into you already. They know you even when you think they don't have a clue. Sometimes we think we have all the answers, when in fact we haven't even finished figuring out all of life's questions. We think we have life all figured out, when in fact, a lot of the time we do not even know ourselves. Our parents are really that safety net for when we misjudge our self. They are anointed to parent us. Dating does not provide this, everyone is pretty much on their own, to figure it out and to work it out.

Let's go back to the story of Isaac and Rebekah when Abraham sat down with his servant and told him to go back to his homeland and find a wife for his son. You can rest assure that Abraham gave his servant specific instructions on what type of wife to bring back for his son, because he knew his son. He knew what type of features he liked, what type of temperament and personality he needed and everything else. The servant knew not to just bring anything back. The Bible says when Rebekah came, Isaac loved her. Really, because she was hand picked specifically for him, by the direction of his father, based on who he was. There had to have been specific requirements involved in the selection that did not cause Rebekah to be a returned bride. When the servant brought Rebekah to Isaac took her as his wife and he loved her.

We will always remember a young man who came to our office to get instructions on how to proceed forward with the courting process with a young lady he believed God wanted him to marry. They met at church and became friends and both moved away. Because they were friends, they remained in contact via e-mail and phone calls. Over the course of time, more began to develop. He decided that she may be the one. The first thing we told him was to respect her father as her covering and talk to him concerning his intentions to court her. We stressed making it clear he was not asking for her hand in marriage, but only his blessing to see her exclusively for the purpose of seeing if they would be compatible for marriage based on who they were and where they felt their life direction was going.

Upon seeing the young lady many months afterwards she told us how well things went, she said her father was so amazed that the young man asked permission to court his daughter and respected his position as her father. (She said none of her sisters before her had done this).

You don't know how many times we have heard "I should have listened". Often times, even if we don't like our parents response it can save a lot of time and heart ache.

ENGAGEMENT

Family is the first institution ordained and established by God in the Garden of Eden. Church, was a result of the fall of man to bring us back into relationship with God. The top three reasons people divorce are; sex, in-laws and finances. To enlist family and in-laws as allies opposed to enemies is of a far greater value, and has far less stress on a marriage than if your family and in-laws are your enemies.

Chances are your future spouse was not raised the same as you. You will have to get used to his or her family the same way that you had to get to know your future spouse. Be patient and give them time and commit to the process. This is a perfect time to recognize and remember that there will likely be many family differences. Engagement is a great time to begin to recognize differences, learn how to accept differences, and work with them. You will have to learn how to embrace both families of origin.

Engagement is a great opportunity to get to know future in-laws better and maybe even members of your own family. I will never forget a young man told us that his family really did not want him to marry the young lady that he was engaged to marry. She never wanted to visit his family and when she did she would sit off to herself and not interact. His sister told him that she was making sure that she did not become connected to them so when she ever got ready divorced him there would be no strings attached that would be difficult to sever. His sister was right she had no accountability or emotional connection with any of his family, not even his mother. So when she decided she wanted a divorce 18 months after the wedding there were few to no connections keeping her in the marriage. It is more than appropriate, it is necessary to get the parents blessing before moving into marriage.

It is important that as couples prepare to go into marriage that they evaluate their involvement with their families. We have seen where young married couples have abandoned their own families and said we are the only family we need now. This is not true at all. One thing we did early in our marriage that we had to rebalance was church becoming our sole family. Any family and vacation time was planned around church events and what was going on at church. If family events and reunions were scheduled during the time of a church event, it was a simple decision, we missed the family event.

Really it wasn't just extended family but even within our own marriage we planned our own lives and needs around church's needs. When we began having children and realized they didn't know many of their cousins and other relatives we recognized we were doing them a disservice and had to find a balance that incorporated all the important aspects of our lives.

Engagement is also a great time to begin looking at how and when you will spend time with your families. The two families will eventually be three families; his family of origin, her family of origin, and the two of you. For example, you both may be accustomed to spending Christmas with your family. When you get married who will you spend time with at Christmas? Easter? Thanksgiving? You will have to consider geographical locations, family size, customs and traditions, and eventually children. It is better to think about and discuss these things before hand about how you will spend your time with family particularly on major holidays

I consider parents and family to be the set up for things to go well for a couple, the built in blessing plan. You have heard it said a thousand times in Sunday School honoring your father and your mother is the only commandment with a promise. There is something to be said of this, particularly for those who are looking to the Word of God and want their marriage and life to go well. Therefore, as you move forward you want to make sure you get their blessing and that your life is well watered from the well of their blessing.

Ask for a young lady's hand in marriage opposed to just taking her from under the covering of her parents. Further, while it is customary for the man to request the hand of the young lady from her father, both parties should know that they have the blessing from both families before proceeding in a life together. We have seen where the man's family, generally the mother, has made it living treachery for the woman because they did not .

We also suggest individuals make sure they make right any areas that they may have dishonored their parents before getting married. If there is one person on earth that will remind us of a parent, particularly if it was an antagonistic relationship, it will be our spouse. We call this designed to grind. This involves two principles from God's Word: sowing and reaping and judgments. Life works by principles of the Kingdom whether we recognize it or not, whether we believe them or not, and whether we know the principles. So pray and ask God to show you anything that may open a door for the enemy to come into your marriage. Whatever you do, just make sure you leave the covering of your parents right before going under someone else's covering, or becoming a covering for someone else. What you do not get right with your parents will follow you into your marriage and will show up in the most unlikely ways.

PART 2

Apply Your Heart To Knowledge
Tools That Will Help Keep You

*Apply thine heart unto instruction, and
thine ears to the words of knowledge.*
Proverbs 23:12

*So that thou incline thine ear unto wisdom,
and apply thine heart to understanding;*
Proverbs 2:2

Again I have always been of the opinion that the cliché "knowledge is power" is just not true. I have heard it all my life and still continue to hear it, but I do not agree with it. After all if I know the stove is hot, yet proceed to put my hand on it, that knowledge apparently was not power to me. This is realized for certain when I get burned. Likewise, many Christians have been burned when they already knew the stove was hot; in fact that the kitchen was hot. They knew not to fornicate, not to do this, and not to do that, but didn't apply what they morally, ethically, spiritually, and, reasonably knew not to do.

It is amazing how many times we think we can handle certain situations. We think we are strong enough because we have the Holy Spirit. But really I think the strength that God has given us is the wisdom in the Holy Spirit to know when to stop and when to turn and walk away from certain situations. The Holy Spirit would not have us flirt with temptations because flesh is weak. We see time and time again so many who experience adverse repercussions for what they knew not to do in the first place. Therefore, is knowing really enough? Apparently it's not.

We, on the other hand, believe that the *application* of knowledge is power. This is called wisdom. Actually doing or applying whatever information that has been received.

We believe that we have to continue to empower the Body of Christ with the *how to's* as much as we do in teaching the *what to's*. Let me give you an example. Growing up in Sunday school it almost seemed like every other Sunday School lesson was about forgiveness. Forgive seven times seventy. I knew that lesson well. Truthfully I understood that I had to forgive those that hurt and offended me. However as I became an adult I realized I knew what I was suppose to do-forgive, but I did not quit understand how to forgive. Many times we may know the right answers, the *what's,* that we should be doing, but are sometimes a little fuzzy concerning the details about the *how's* for doing the what.

This second section is about just that, the *how to's.* It is about empowerment through practical and meaningful ways to honor your commitment to prepare yourself and your decision to "be kept". As we mentioned in the beginning of the book it was a decision of ours to be kept. The decision by itself was the easy part, but truthfully it by itself was not enough. Yes, sticking to that decision took God, but it also took us actually doing practical things we knew to do. As we shared it can be done.

In Part II we talk about the practical human efforts on your part, coupled with all the biblical truths, spiritual revelation and information you know. In other words, apply your heart to instruction, knowledge and understanding.

CHAPTER 7

Mirror, Mirror
(4 C's Of Getting to Know You)

This one chapter is the brick and mortar on the framework of your decision. It is very crucial. "To thy own self be true" is what comes to mind. It is not enough to know yourself, but you must also like who you are and love yourself.

However, we believe for individuals to really know who they are they must first know who God is. He is the one that has exclusively designed each of us, He knows what's in us, how we operate, and He knows our destiny and desires. We have to connect with Him to connect with all of that is inside of us. When we know who He is, according to the Word, then, and only then, will we be able to identify the power within us to do exploits. God has called each of us to greatness, in some capacity. Locked up within each of us is great ability waiting to be unleashed.

Furthermore, I am unable to know someone else until I really know me. Through knowing and having understanding of who I am, I can begin to understand what will fit and what will not fit in my life, and for my life. This is critical because relationships become unstable, for everyone involved, when someone has to go look for them self. Have it resolved who you are, and make sure in the courting process the other party has resolved who they are.

Often times in life we have so many other peoples stuff and issues on us that we never get down to who we really are. We can be compared to an onion. My favorite onions are Vidalia and Bermuda. Onions are probably one of the most flavorful and potent vegetables we use to flavor food. However we have yet to see anyone through in a whole onion or cut one up into a recipe without first removing the fine layers of skin. Your eyes well up with tears and it is somewhat of a task to remove the skin. However to get the full intended flavor each tiny thin little layer has to be peeled off. Likewise to get down to who God has intended us to be, who we really are, we have to allow God to peel all the tiny thin layers off of us. These layers represent what was said and done *to* us as much as they represent what was not said and done *for* us. They represent year's of other people's issues, problems, and words on us. However when the layers of other peoples opinions and issues are peeled off of us then people can enjoy our real flavor. More than that, as you get down to your true self, who you really are, than you will like you. You know how we know that? Because, God likes you.

We have included 4 areas for knowing yourself before moving forward with knowing someone else. We call them the 4 C's of Knowing You. Make sure you are resolved in your spirit about these four areas before proceeding to the altar.

1) **Complete** in Christ

Know God for yourself. Make sure you have a personal relationship with Christ. Be sure He is not only Savior but He is also Lord. Know His voice, follow it, and know that when you need to get through to Him you can.

In like manner make sure that you live conscience of the work of Calvary on a daily basis. Forgive others, and keep your heart right. Far too often people walk around with unresolved issues and hurts of the past incarcerated in their heart. Until you release others and forgive them they will always have a certain amount of occupancy in your heart and your life. It will show up in your actions, behaviors, and attitudes. It will affect your marriage and your other relationships. Forgive quickly. Always examine your own heart to make sure you are in right standing, not just "right". Honor and respect from a truthful heart and not out of obligation.

2.) **Content** With Who You Are

Have a healthy self image. The best way we can think to say it is "like you". With that, respect yourself. Understand that very few people in life will discern your worth at a greater value than what you assign to yourself. Very few people will just treat you better than how you treat yourself. Take care of yourself, and carry yourself in a manner worthy of dignity and respect. For those relationships that do not discern the same value that you assign to yourself then those are the relationships that you need to cut loose.

Know your strengths and weaknesses as you remember you are a work in progress. Know what you want in life and what you do not want out of life. With this information be aware of distractions that come to keep you from purpose.

3.) **Called**, on your way somewhere

Have a vision (goals, dreams, aspirations). The vision referred to in Proverbs 29:18 acts as an ark of safety. God has not put us here to live to work, and work to live. We are ambassadors for the Kingdom of Heaven and God has a specific assignment for each one of us. Discover your destiny and why you have been created. As you are busy fulfilling and equipping yourself for purpose chances are you will find someone doing the same. Those sitting around doing nothing waiting for their prince/princess aren't likely to attract a spouse going in the same direction. Allow God's vision for your life to be the light that directs your path.

4.) **Confident** that God's will for your life is good

Even greater than how you see yourself is how God sees you. Knowing how He sees you begin to see the things that He has planned for you. Jeremiah 29 reminds us that His will for our life is good and He has a hope and a future and an expected end for each of us. And it's good. Regardless of what things look like around you remember the promise God has given you and remember He will bring it to pass in your life as you are aligned.

CHAPTER 8

Watch It
(8 Ways to Remain)

Wherewithal shall a young man cleanse his way?
by taking heed thereto according to thy word.
Psalms 119:9

Enough really cannot be said about this scripture. Neither can we say it any better than how it has already been written. Take heed to the word of God, and it will keep you. The word heed implies going beyond being aware, but implies several things even greater. Remember it's not knowledge that is power, but what you do with the knowledge you have been given. To heed says to build a hedge around something for the purpose of protecting it and attending to it. It also implies observing, not in the sense of seeing, but rather in actually doing.

God has laid out for us, within the principles of His Word, everything we need to live a successful life. Jesus Christ Himself is that living Word that lives within us. We simply have to take due diligence and pull these principals out of God's Word as though they are precious gems that will make our lives rich. Our confidence is, He that lives in us is mighty, and we too have that same power and might, through Him, to do what He has purposed for us.

With this, one thing we have learned over the years in the midst of Christian-dom is the power of balance. Why? God is concerned with every aspect of our lives. Not just the Sunday morning me, but the Monday through Sunday me. If He can only move on my behalf Sunday morning for a couple of hours I need something else that is going to work on Tuesday evening or Thursday afternoon. But that is not God. He is concerned with all the details pertaining to us all the time. He knows our dreams and aspirations, and He wants to see them fulfilled in our life. He knows the kind of career you want, the kind of spouse you want, and its okay with Him. Remember He knows all about you. He created you. Right? Our dreams are just God's ideas in us. Therefore we can live above board with what we want, desire and dream. So we say most definitely, He wants the best for you because His will for your life is GOOD!

*For I know the thoughts that I think towards
you, saith the Lord, thoughts of peace, and
not of evil, to give you an expected end.*
Jeremiah 29:11

Eight is the number of new beginnings. Here we have listed eight practical ways to help the believer maintain their character and integrity. They are unique in that they fit everyone; they are not gender or age specific. In other words they are not just for youth, but will help the adults as well. They are not just for the ladies, but are very fitting for gentlemen too.

We often times remind people of what you are told by the flight attendant right before take off. They tell you that in the event of cabin de-oxygenation place the oxygen mask over your own face before you help someone else. The same applies with this chapter. If you try to help someone else before you actually get it you both may become casualties. The best two ways to use the *8 Ways to Remain Pure* is to first make sure you practice them, and second avoid relationships with those who do not respect them.

1.) **Make the choice**

*I call heaven and earth to record this day against you, that I have set before
you life and death, blessing and cursing: therefore choose life, that both thou
and thy seed may live:* (Deuteronomy 30:19)

Choose to remain pure and commit to that decision before getting involved in relationships. Cultivate this decision before the time comes for you to rely on it. Study the Word, pray, and fast build up your spiritual man on a daily basis. When the time comes He will reveal that right person for you. He will also identify the counterfeits to you.

2.) **Have a life**

*…I am come that they might have life, and that they might have it more
abundantly.* (John 10:10)

Monitor the amount of time spent together. We could stress this point a thousand times over. You're only committed to God. Far too often when people decide to get involved they think that means being together 24/7; every waking minute. Their only time apart is to go home, sleep and shower. When they are not together they are either speaking on the phone or sleeping on the phone. We say to you have a life and have relevant relationships with other people.

Have a life; otherwise there is a tendency to rely on, and expect someone else to become your life. This is too much stress and pressure to put on anyone. On the other hand, while it may be flattering, at first, it is too much stress and pressure for you to allow anyone to put on you. It is out of balance and unbiblical for anyone to be your world. That is Jesus' position.

Through counseling we have found it to be self damaging when someone assumes the savior role in a relationship. What happens is everything gets attributed to this one person. Subconsciously life revolves around him or her. If the sun is shinning, and all is going well it's because that person is so wonderful. If it is a storm in their life, and nothing seems to be going right, it becomes their fault—and they become responsible to fix it. Only Jesus can quiet the storm.

Find what you like to do, and do it, then keep doing it. It will add depth and dimension to a relationship to be able to share your interests with another person, whether those interest are common or different.

3.) Have relevant relationships

> *Where no counsel is, the people fall: but in the multitude of counselors there is safety.* (Proverbs 11:14)

The word relevant actually comes from a Latin word meaning to lift again. It also points to the idea of mattering to the point of making a difference. Relationships help make our lives richer by the connections we share with one another. Each of us should continue to develop and cherish the relationships in our life that intrinsically make a difference by adding to us and lifting us up.

4.) Avoid situations/conversations that are physical or sexual in nature

> *Finally, brethren, whatsoever things are true, whatsoever things are honest, whatsoever things are just, whatsoever things are pure, whatsoever things are lovely, whatsoever things are of good report: if there be any virtue, and if there be any praise, think on these things.* (Philippians 4:8)

One of the easiest ways of making something happen is to start playing games. Watch what you say and don't play games. There should just be some *don't go there* conversations that you just do not engage in with those of the opposite sex. Have some sense of propriety about yourself in terms of what is appropriate and what is inappropriate.

5.) **Avoid physical contact**

Can a man take fire in his bosom, and his clothes not be burned? (Proverbs 6:27)

There was a lot of wisdom in what the older mothers use to say. "There is no need to buy the cow if the milk is free." A touch goes a long way, and for some it has led them to go all the way. Think about it if the very presence of someone gives you goose bumps, the smell of their cologne/perfume gives you tingles, how do you think your body will react if you're holding hands, chewing on ears, breathing down necks, or rubbing backs, shoulders, and various body parts? Once your physical body experiences the sensation of certain touches your mind and body collaborate together to reenact, recapture, simulate, and stimulate those initial feelings again.

6.) **Use modesty in dressing**

Let all things be done decently and in order. (I Corinthians14:40)

This is a tricky one, but not really. This applies to both genders, not just the ladies. I guess what was once obvious has become a very grey and very shaded area because so much has become acceptable across the board. We know God is not running around with a ruler to measure hem lines, neck lines and mid drifts, but have some sense of modesty about your self. Clothes speak a language all by their self that can suggest what your mouth may never say. Evaluate the message your clothes are sending.

7.) **Avoid private prayer meetings**

Abstain from all appearance of evil. (I Thessalonians 5:22)

We have to be careful that our good is not evil spoken of, in whatever we do. We don't want to give the appearance of evil, but be an example of what is good and upright. Having too many dates alone is not necessarily a good idea, particularly when it is at one of your homes. There have been a lot of children conceived through these private prayer meetings. Something is much less likely to happen when a third party is present.

8.) **Refrain from playing house**

Discretion shall preserve thee, understanding shall keep thee: (Proverbs 2:11)

The older mothers use to also say "don't play house until you get a house". The term *discreet* denotes having *a* sense of deliberate prudence and precaution about one's actions and conversations. This is relevant in terms of if you are single than be single. Making married decisions, once again without the commitment of marriage, can come back to bite you. Making married decisions takes on many forms, which really may be done out of innocence or ignorance. We've found this to be far more common than what we previously thought i.e. sharing accounts, finances, raising kids, etc.

Many times this is where soul ties are strengthened if not developed, outside of sexual relationships, particularly when it comes to finances. Christians have come to know soul ties primarily in the area of sexual relationship, but that is really just the tip of the iceberg. Let's look at why.

Remember our soul consists of three parts; our mind, heart, and will. Let's look at each aspect. The heart is the seat of our emotions and feelings. This is often the area that gets us in trouble. The Bible says *"where your treasure is there your heart will be also" (Matthew 6:21)*. It also says *"the heart is deceitful above all things, and desperately wicked…" (Jeremiah 17:9)*.

Another area of our soul is our *mind*. *This* area consists of or intellect and thinking processes. The Word of God clearly says *"Let this mind be in you, as it was also in Christ Jesus:" (Philippians 2:5)*.

The final area of our soul is our *will*. This is where our choices and decisions get acted on and played out. That thing which I desire to do I don't do, and that which I don't desire to do I do. Sound familiar? The power behind will is so strong that it pays to harness it and make it subject to the Lord Jesus Christ in your life.

Do you see where we are going with this? When we intertwine the most personal aspects of our being with another person we are tying ourselves to that person. So where there may not have been a sexual relationship, my money being your money, you raising my children, and the like will tie us together in a potentially deceitful and wicked way. This type of oneness is reserved for when the two become one through marriage.

CHAPTER 9

Six Promises To Keep
(With Yourself)

Where there is no vision, the people perish:
But he that keepeth the law, happy is he.
Proverbs 29:18(KJV)

Where there is no revelation the people
cast off restraint.
Proverbs 29:18 (NIV))

After you know God and what He wants for your life then you can begin to set goals that will take you in that direction. Only when we know where we are going can we make plans that actually get us there. Vision gives us this direction and focus. It lets us know what direction we are going in. Vision acts as a safeguard that gives us parameters and margins that keep us within the boundaries of the road that takes us toward our goals. Because I know there is a certain place I am trying to get to, I begin to understand there are certain things that I will have to do to reach my goal. Likewise there are certain things that I cannot do that would keep me from reaching my goal. We call these things distractions. Distractions come in all sizes, shapes, shades, and heights. Relationships are one of the major reasons people take detours outside of the margins and parameters that lead them to their goals and destiny. As these distractions come, and they will, I absolutely have to remember my vision and maintain my focus so that I get to where both God, and I, want me to be.

Six is the number of man. This is what Chapter 9, Six Promises to Keep (With Yourself), the final chapter, is about. They are promises for you to make with yourself to help keep you focused. We do not only want you to obtain but also maintain all of God's promises and benefits for your life. Become familiar with the six promises and as life situations present themselves, remember to thy own self be true.

1) <u>Purpose</u>: *I promise to walk out my purpose.*

[I] a4m his workmanship, created in Christ Jesus unto good works...
(Ephesians 2:10)

- I am here because I have been created for a special purpose.
- The bigger picture of my life is independent of if I ever get married or not.

2) <u>Person</u>: *I Promise to be who God has called me to be.*

[I] am a chosen generation, a royal priesthood, and a holy nation (1 Peter 2:9)

- My value is from being created by God and in His image.
- Recognize and remember you are in Christ.
- You are created the way God desired you to be.
- You are created in the image and likeness of God and already have within you all things that pertain to life and godliness. You are equipped to look and act like Him.

3) <u>Property</u>: *I promise to only belong to God.*

[I] was made by him (John 1:3) and for him.

- I belong to God. Not to my self or to anyone else.

4) <u>Preparation</u>: *I promise to prepare myself for where God is taking me and for what God has given me to do.*

He which hath begun a good work in [me] will perform it until the day of Jesus Christ. (Philpippians1:6)

- I will prepare myself for all God wants to do in my life.
- Singleness is a great opportunity to maximize me; to prepare and better myself, and head toward destiny for my life.

5) <u>Peace</u>: *I promise that God will be my place of peace.*

Thou will keep [me] in perfect peace, whose mind is stayed on thee: because [I] trust in thee. (Isaiah 26:3)

- I will keep my eyes on God and not be distracted by what's happening around me.
- He is my peace on those see nothing days
- Happy is he who keeps the law.

6) <u>Process</u>: *I promise to go through the processes of life.*

Yeah, though I walk through the valley of the shadow of death, I will fear no evil... (Psalms 23:4)

- There will be times of testing in my life, but it is to perfect me, not to kill me. God will bring me out every time.
- I will stay my course and finish the race set for me.

Our Desire For You

Our desire for you is the same, we believe, as God's desire for you. We pray that if you desire to marry that God will reveal who that special someone is. We even know where you will find her, or where he will find you-in the Kingdom! Don't limit yourself and definitely don't limit God. What God has for you is for you, and this person can be anyplace.

Remember God's will for your life is good. He wants to give you an expected end; a future and a hope. Therefore, remember to prepare yourself, not just for marriage, but for your Kingdom purpose. Partner with God and He will fulfill your desires. Commit your ways to Him, and He will direct your paths. When He brings that person to you, you will experience the assurance that a three fold cord is not easily broken. He won't disappoint you!

If you are one of those who feel like you have blown your chance, because maybe you got involved prematurely, went beyond the boundaries, you just did not know, or whatever the case, always remember the cross is about reconciliation and redemption. He has already forgiven you, now you forgive you, and start from today. Remember His will for your life is good, without exception. I think you will like His will for you.

For those of you who may say, this marriage thing is not for me, well, so be it. To you I say advance the Kingdom. If by chance you change your mind later, keep doing what you're doing with the help He brings along side of you.

Contact Information

To contact Frank and Lisa Armstead

To Inquire About
Further Materials; or
For An Itinerary

P.O. Box 30413
Pensacola, FL 32503
KDMInternational@aol.com
(850)358-9548